A Builder of the
New South

A Builder of the New South

Notes on the career of Thomas M. Logan

Lily Logan Morrill

Edited By Stewart W. Bentley, Jr., PhD

authorHOUSE®

AuthorHouse™
1663 Liberty Drive
Bloomington, IN 47403
www.authorhouse.com
Phone: 1-800-839-8640

First published by AuthorHouse   11/12/2011

ISBN: 978-1-4678-7033-7 (sc)
ISBN: 978-1-4678-7032-0 (ebk)

Printed in the United States of America

Contents

Introduction to the Authorhouse Edition

General Thomas M. Logan was a man of his times and a man ahead of his time. Coming of age during the American Civil War, he possessed many of the same traits as other Americans of the 19th Century. At the same time, following the turmoil and bloodshed of the War, Logan emerged with a new appreciation of what the United States could become and did not pine for what could have been.

This work, edited by his daughter, Lily Logan Morrill, captures the first clash of arms, the aftermath of the War, and the building of both the Logan family and the General's contribution to rebuilding the South. Logan understood that rebuilding the South meant that change would have to occur; not only societal, but political and economic changes that would help the South reintegrate into the United States and strengthen the country as a whole.

The story provides us with a unique insight into the life of Thomas and Kate Logan as they struggled to survive the War, adjust to the outcome and move forward towards a New South.

I am indebted again to Sarah Donnelly and her family for permission to reprint this work and for Sarah's painstaking proofreading of the draft.

Preface

T here are three reasons for writing this, the first full-length, documented biography of General Thomas M. Logan of the Confederate Army. He was one of the most brilliant as well as youngest brigadier in the war between the States, he was a prime mover in the rehabilitation of the South, and he was one of the early major railroad builders in that section of the country.

Thomas Muldrup Logan was born in Charleston, South Carolina, in November, 1840. When he was just over twenty years old, in December of 1860, he was graduated from South Carolina College at the top of his class. South Carolina was then the scene of great excitement, being the first state to secede from the Union. Logan ardently espoused the cause of Secession, and in less than six months saw active service during the siege of Fort Sumter. After the surrender of the Fort, he and a few friends organized a company of their own, Company A, Hampton Legion Infantry. Logan was elected Second Lieutenant, declining any higher rank. But his rise was to be very rapid. He was in the thick of the fight about Manassas, and for his heroism was elected captain.

Covering these first days of the War, I have made use of many hitherto unpublished letters, giving minute details of the camp life of this company. These letters take Logan through the first year of the war. From then on, material is drawn from various other sources both published and unpublished. The most useful of these is the new edition of the Record of the Logan Family, gotten up by me under my father's supervision. I have also drawn from informal pamphlets, family accounts, and journalistic records.

The importance of General Logan as a military man is fully attested by the following official communications:

Headquarters, 1st Corps, A.N.V.

December 13, 1864.

General:

Colonel Logan of the Hampton Legion, Gary's Brigade, was in my command from July, 1862, until about March, 1864, when his regiment was transferred to the Cavalry Service. I was particularly attracted by his skill and gallantry in the pursuit of the enemy (in November, 1863) from London to Knoxville, where on two occasions he charged and routed a line of battle with his skirmish line. He also particularly distinguished himself in the affair at Dandridge, East Tennessee, in January last. More recently he has been under my command as Colonel of the Carolina Regiment and as Senior Colonel commanding Gary's Brigade, in both of which capacities his conduct has merited my warmest approbation. He has always proved himself a very cool, skillful and gallant officer, and I most cordially recommend his early promotion to the position of Brigadier General. I am, General,

> Very respectfully,
> your most obedient servant,
> **(Signed) J. Longstreet,**
> Lieutenant General.

To General S. Cooper,
A.J.S. General, Richmond, VA

> Headquarters Butler's
> Cavalry Division
> Hicksford, January 6th, 1865.

General S. Cooper,
Adjutant and Inspector General,
Richmond, Virginia.
General:

I have the honor to request that Colonel T.M. Logan be promoted to the rank of Brigadier General and assigned to my old brigade of the division. It is sufficient for me to say of Colonel Logan that he has always had the confidence of his superior officers, and I refer the Department with confidence to the opinions of General Robert E. Lee, Lieutenant General Longstreet, Lieutenant General Ewell, Major General Hampton, and Brigadier General

Gary as to his qualifications for command. He is one of those young men who has risen to his present position from a lieutenancy by devotion to the cause, earnestness of purpose, attention to duty, military capacity and personal gallantry, and I most respectfully urge his appointment, and ask his assignment to the brigade indicated, as it is very much in need of an experienced officer.

I have the honor, General, to be

Most respectfully,
Your most obedient
servant, M.C. Butler,
Major General.

The following are endorsements by Generals Hampton and Lee, found on Butler's letter just given:

Headquarters Army
of Northern Virginia
January 9th, 1865.

Respectfully forwarded and recommend. I believe Colonel Logan the best appointment that can be made for this brigade, and I request his promotion at once.

(Signed) R.E. Lee, General
(F.L. 347)

Official: John W. Riely, A.A.G

Headquarters Cavalry.
January 6th, 1865.

Respectfully forwarded application. I have already recommended Colonel Logan for promotion, as I regard him as one of the very best officers of his rank in the service.

(Signed) Wade Hampton,
Major General.

Shortly after the War, General Logan concentrated his attention on healing the wounds of conflict. Writing in Harper's Magazine in March, 1876, he said: "With such an industrial outlook for the South, it is time that childish despondency makes way for manly energy; it is time that vain lamentations over the past yield to hopeful anticipations of the future; it is time that false forebodings of coming evil give place to honest efforts for the common good."

Speaking before the Reunion of Hood's Texas Brigade at Waco, Texas, June, 1876, he said: "No nation has ever been permanently established without some bonds of union to hold it together. There must be social cohesion, whether resulting from past associations and the attachments of a common ancestry, or future hopes and the sympathy of a common destiny . . . What folly, then, to talk of antagonism in this country between Puritan and Cavalier politics! The struggle between the Federal and State authority will continue;

but it need not divide a country along geographical lines."

The General felt that these two objectives, building up the South and pulling down sectional prejudices, could best be obtained through improvements in education, including the education of the negro. He said: "All of the arguments usually advanced in favor of public instruction apply with greater force to the negro. And thus every consideration of the subject leads to the conclusion that the future welfare and prosperity of the South demand the education of the freedman by public school instruction."

One way to draw the South out of her depression, General Logan thought, was to build up her railways. As early as April 10, 1872, he wrote an editorial in the Richmond Enquirer, with the imposing title of "Railroads, the Arteries and Veins of the Body Politic." Two years later in the Manchester, Virginia Courier, his subject was "The Railroad Interests of Richmond." Before the seventies the General was already president of the Port Walthall Branch of the Richmond and Petersburg Railroad and soon after that he was Counsel for the Richmond and Danville. With the coming of the 1880s, Logan became more and more ambitious for extending the Richmond and Danville beyond State lines. He succeeded for a time. Then in 1883 wily men in Wall Street shoved him off the railroad map. But this defeat did not discourage him. By what was called a "master stroke" he later again obtained control of the road with greatly increased mileage, which mean increased usefulness to the South.

My sources for every line in this biography are indicated in the chapter notes and bibliography in the back. A very large part of them are here employed for the first time, since they are in form of manuscripts in my possession or in the form of obscure pamphlets, leaflets, and handouts long lost to the public eye. A word about the conversations in the book. Many of them are culled from Logan's own speeches or other writings. Elsewhere they are not meant to be taken literally, but their general authenticity may be relied upon, for they are based on my own memory of the events described, or upon the memories of relatives and friends whom I have consulted over a period of years.

I have also tried to present a picture of the family life both in Richmond and on the farm at Algoma, which I knew first hand. I believe these domestic notes contribute toward a better understanding of life in those times.

Especial acknowledgement is due to Mr. Charles Woodward Hutson who kindly lent me his war correspondence.

Lily Logan Morrill

Chapter I

Boyhood and Youth
1840-1861

On the last day of July, 1850, three little brothers, eight, nine and eleven years old, were fishing in a lazy creek which ran through Mellbrook plantation in South Carolina. This time they had gone to the creek not of their own volition, but because they had nowhere else to go. They were not wanted at home on account of Mother's illness. They couldn't understand it. When Mother had been ill before, the worse she had felt, the more she wanted them around to wait on her and fetch a shawl or smelling salts. Besides, Edward, Mully and Frank were puzzled why their younger sisters had been allowed to remain at home.

The fish were refusing to bite, so Edward and Frank waded out into the water, shouting for Mully to join them. But Mully couldn't shake off the thought of his ailing mother. "Come on, let's go home!" he said.

But at home something had happened that made Mully's head spin, even though he didn't know what it was all about. The little boys clung tearfully together. They would never see Mother again-so Mawmee, their nurse, had said.

Mully was Thomas Muldrup Logan, later General Logan of the Confederate Army, and a leader in building up the New South-especially its railroads. He was born in 1840 in Charleston, South Carolina, the tenth child of Judge George William and Anna D'Oyley Logan. He passed his childhood there, at one of the family homes in Colleton County, that rich "Low Country" nearby, and at Mellbrook, three miles away. His mother had to care for fifteen children, not to mention the many slaves, cutting out every garment they wore with her slender, skilled fingers. Even so she found leisure in which to study and write poetry. Among her poems is this little prayer:

"Lord, ere I close my eyes this night

Help me to raise my thoughts to Thee;

Help me to strive with all my might

My errors to correct and see.

My actions may I scan with care;

Each evil thought and word perceive;

Of unkind words let me beware,

Nor let my self-love me deceive.

Oh, that my days may long proclaim

Love over all my actions reign!

My God, to whom this prayer is said

Oh, may it not be said in vain!"

Little Margaret Polk, only five years old, died shortly after her mother. Mully was too young to appreciate fully the loss of mother and sister, for his time was taken up with his inseparable companions, the two brothers, Francis Glover, now eleven, and Joseph Edward, eight. There was the excitement of moving, too, for Judge Logan, finding familiar surroundings too reminiscent of his lost wife, decide to take the family from South Carolina to New Orleans.

They had been living in New Orleans for several months when the Judge, with his three youngest sons, went to stay with his brother Samuel, near Carrollton, Louisiana. After a short visit Judge Logan started back to the city, accompanied by his sons and five slaves. They drove to the levee which winds in and out, turning the New Orleans riverside into the shape of a double crescent or, more accurately, an "S". The boys' aunt, Mrs. Samuel Logan, who had accompanied them thus far, decided to finish her part of the trip to New Orleans by driving in her barouche along the levee. But Francis, Mully and Edward were to accompany their father in a skiff which was moored nearby.

Impatient to embark, the boys chattered to each other and to the birds in the rustic cages they were carrying as souvenirs of their visit to Uncle Sam's. Soon the boat was ready and the eager lads took their places. The Mississippi was peaceful. The only break in the glassy surface was made by the gentle strokes of the oars which stirred up miniature whirlpools with each dip of the paddle. Edward rubbed his eyes sleepily. He snuggled down under the shade of a big umbrella in the stern. Soon he was fast asleep, his head with its close-cropped golden curls resting on one arm, the other clasping his birdcage. Francis was wide awake but silent, sitting in the front of the boat so as to see everything and be the first to land when they arrived.

When the rocking of the skiff caused Mully's long hair to fly about his face he pushed it back impatiently, envying his brothers their more comfortable short locks. He was planning how best to persuade Sister Lizzie to cut those bothersome curls, when the boat shuddered violently and a moment later he was in the chilly water.

He felt himself being pulled down, down, with the water roaring in his ears. The rest was a blur. He rose to the surface again. His head kept hitting something hard. From afar off he seemed to hear shrieks of terror, and then was brought to by an agonizing wrench. Those same despised curls had become a life line by which he was dragged to shore, still too weak and dazed to ask what had become of his brothers and his father.

Mully's brother Sam, standing on the levee where the boat was supposed to land, saw the accident.

Near the river bank was a half-submerged raft of logs chained together. As the foremost logs were under water they could not be seen and the Logans' boat struck them with a heavy impact. The current sucked the boat and all who were in it deep underneath the raft. Sam, sensing danger as they approached the logs, had signaled in vain to his father to steer around and land farther away from the raft. Mully and his father were both saved by their long hair. The last Mully saw of his little brothers, Edward and Francis, was two golden heads bobbing on the muddy surface of the river for an instant before they were sucked under the waters for the last time-the two little brothers whom he had thought he would always have.

The Logan family went back to Charleston where Mully attended school. In March, 1854, he wrote to his oldest brother George:

My Dear Brother:

I am very glad to hear that you are a Father now and I am an Uncle. I have not written to you for a very long time, and I will give you a description of all that is going on here now. I went to a party last night given by Miss Cicelia Englesby. It was a pretty large one. We left at 11 o'clock.-I would be much obliged if you would send me one of those butterfly or Crane kites; for there are none of them here. If you can, send one or two by the next vessel. The boys out here, I don't think, have ever seen one of them. A blind man has been preaching in the Unitarian church. He has a Bible made of raised letters so that he can read with his fingers; and nobody could read it but himself. Some of them tried but could not. He has to read very slowly, certainly, but you can understand him. Mr. Belcher, my drawing teacher, has gone to the North to get a few things for his drawing school and also some books for his common school. I suppose that he will be back in a couple of weeks. I practice drawing every leisure moment I have. When are you going to come out and see us, and bring your little babe. I don't suppose that you have named her yet. All send love to you and sister, and all our friends and relations in Louisiana. I remain as always your truly affec brother.

Mully.

Mully, his sisters said, was always ambitious to study and learn. He also felt an obligation toward Charleston and South Carolina, for he knew that his forbears had done their part in the development of the Colony.

The first American settler of his branch was Colonel George Logan of His Majesty's Army, who embarked from Aberdeen and arrived in Charleston in 1690. He soon became prominent for he was in command of a troop of horse in 1706, when Charleston was invaded by the Spaniards and French.

In 1716 he was "Speaker" of the Provincial House, and as such his name heads the list of a large number of Representatives who addressed a "bold memorial" to the King of England (George I) complaining of the tyranny and ill government of the Lords Proprietors.

ii He left two children, a daughter, Helen, and George, who married Martha Daniell. Martha's father, Robert Daniell, the friend and associate of Colonel George Logan and Mully's ancestor in the maternal line, also came to Charleston about the year 1690, probably in company with Colonel Logan. Later Daniell was made Governor of South Carolina.

Martha Daniell Logan was distinguished in her own right, for she was one of the earliest horticulturists in this country. She and Bartram carried on a lively correspondence, quote in Darlington's Memoirs of John Bartram. Bailey, in his encyclopedia, mentions her Gardener's Kalendar, which is also spoken of in Mrs. St. Julien Ravenel's "Charleston, the Place and the People," in "Old Time Gardens," by Alice Moss Earle, and in the South Carolina Historical Magazine.

From great-great grandmother Martha Logan, Mully may have inherited his love of beauty. From other ancestors he might also have inherited a gift for healing had he cared to exercise it. His great grandfather and his grandfather (both Georges) were well known physicians. Besides accomplishing distinguished work as a surgeon, the later George Logan wrote a popular work of about three hundred pages on "The Diseases of Children." Mully was named for a third physician, his Uncle Thomas Muldrup Logan, later well known in Sacramento, California. But as his brother Samuel had decided to practice medicine in New Orleans, Mully at an early age elected to study law.

At Lessesene' School in Charleston he progressed so rapidly that at sixteen he was able to enter the sophomore class of Charleston College. He soon transferred to South Carolina College at Columbia where he was graduated in December, 1860, first in a class of forty. His flaming will to do must have come from the Danish ancestress, Honoria Muldrup. His Scottish forbears may have added steady energy, business ability and capacity for culture.

During his college life in Columbia he attended social[iii] gatherings freely and enjoyed them. On one occasion, where there were tableaux, one of them represented the Sleeping Beauty waked from her enchantment by the kiss of the Prince. Mully was chosen to enact the part of the Prince, and the Beauty was a handsome and cultivated Jewess. The kiss was not heard and, I dare say, was only simulated. They were Victorian in those days.

A classmate, C.W. Hutson, tells another story about young Mully. It concerns a tight lipped lady who favored her own daughter socially to the neglect of her stepdaughter, a lovely and gentle girl. Mully conspired with his comrades to boom the neglected sister, who from then on never missed a dance. This incident was characteristic of Logan, whose own early grief made him deplore all suffering.

But life was not all gallantry for Mully Logan. He often went to the room of a classmate, Charles W. Hutson, a favorite meeting place for students. There the group had many earnest discussions until late into the night. Much of their talk centered around the increasing friction between the North and the South. How could this be otherwise in South Carolina, where sectional bitterness was fast reaching its climax?

Mully was sufficiently thoughtful to realize that the state of tension had not come all at once, but had been growing for years. He had taken a great interest in the Stephen A. Douglas campaign, and followed with a keen eye all the exciting events of the Constitutional Convention in his own city, in April, 1860. He had been surrounded by intense partisan and thus his young mind had agreed entirely with the Southern delegations who had "come to Charleston with one great purpose[iv]-'to save our Constitutional rights, if it lay in our power to do so'".

When Alabama bolted the convention and was later followed by Mully's own state, South Carolina, the young student's mind was made up. If all this meant war, then it would be his duty to battle for the Southern Cause-the cause of Constitutionality and States' Rights. Anyway that was how secession was looked upon by the young men of Charleston. They had thought they could slip out quietly from the Union. If that proved impossible, they were going to escape by other means. If they could not leave by the side door they were willing to meet the gruff policeman at the front entrance and make a bold fight for freedom.

Chapter II

War Begins
1861-1863

I n December, 1860, when South Carolina came to the front as the first state to secede from the Union, Mully Logan enlisted as a private in the Washington Light Infantry. Dark haired and slender in his new grey uniform; he was very serious and dignified for his twenty years, looking almost too young for a full fledged soldier. But his boyhood days were behind him. He had been recently graduated from South Carolina College and was ready to shoulder a man's burden. The very mold of his handsome features, the keen blue eyes, high, broad forehead, resolute, full lips presaged the force of character that was to distinguish him later for salient qualities of generalship-vision, quick thinking and a capacity for rapid decisions and constructive action on the field of battle. Already he was evolving a philosophy of life, not the bravery of callousness but the Spartan acceptance of reality. It was from this beginning that he developed his taste for Epictetus and Marcus Aurelius by whose dictates he strove to mould his later years. Later, he often told his children: "We can bear anything! The pain of one instant is not realized until the next. By then, it is over."

On April 4th, 1861, the Charleston morning paper spoke of a suspicious schooner, which when it tried to pass the Morris Island battery, was fired upon and put back. This was the beginning of the trouble which ended in the siege of Fort Sumter eight days later. The Southern officer, Beauregard, demanded that Major Anderson evacuate the fort because the people of Charleston resented the presence of Northern troops in their midst. When Anderson refused to leave, the Confederates turned their guns on Sumter. The Northerners fired in return and the War Between the States was on. The whole city was awakened by the bombardment. Strange to say, no one was killed, although the fighting lasted thirty-four hours. In the end Anderson capitulated, hauling down his tattered red flag. At this acknowledgement of defeat the Charlestonians went wild with joy. The victorious Commander, Beauregard, became the hero of the hour. Logan and his friends who had served in the battle with a Militia Company-the Washington Light Infantry-were full of enthusiasm for him and the Southern Cause.

After the surrender of the Fort, Mully and his companions organized a company for active service and invited Captain James Conner to cooperate. With the help of Conner's influential name the complement of men was soon obtained and Logan was elected Second Lieutenant, declining a higher rank. The

Company was mustered into the Confederate service as Company A., Hampton Legion Infantry.[v]

By this time Georgia, Alabama, Florida, Mississippi, Louisiana and Texas had already joined the Confederacy; Virginia followed soon after; then came Arkansas, Tennessee and North Carolina. Mully's South Carolina "Bonnie Blue Flag which bears a single Star" was no longer the emblem of the whole Confederacy because each State as it came in added its own star.

There is extant a note written by Kate Cox of Virginia to her brother Edwin, on May 7th, 1861. Her letter paper is marked with the new Confederate flag-two red bars across with a white one in between. The upper corner, near the staff, is a blue field with seven white stars. Some of the later seceding states were not yet shown on the flag.

Clover Hill, Virginia
May 7th, 1861

"Yes, my brother, go to work with all your heart, soul and strength, fearing God but not dreading what man may do. The news of your departure for Norfolk made a sensation in our little family circle as you may well imagine-but that is over now and tho' we all feel anxious, we would not have you away from the place your country has called you to fill-be it even at the cannon's mouth or bayonet's point."

Such was the spirit with which the whole South-men and women-entered the war. These were no idle words; they were proved sincere by the hardest of tests during four long years.

On the eighth of June, Mully, now a Lieutenant, went with the Hampton Legion to Camp Hampton, near Columbia, South Carolina. This company was first in the field, the others not having yet arrived. Their tents were soon pitched and everything arranged. In those days soldiers were allowed, in their letters home, to specify their exact location, and Columbia was their post office.[vi] The men drilled frequently. General James Conner said in May, "The Company is a very fine one and I intend to make it the crack company of the regiment."

There was little shade in the neighborhood, so Mully and his friends contrived an arbor of oak boughs, which gave them a cool spot on which to recline during their many leisure moments. On rainy days they kept dry in their tents by using shawls and blankets as much as the heat and crowding allowed. The fare was not very inviting, but they managed occasional visits to Columbia where they purchased more appetizing supplies.

Refreshments also came from their many friends. Mrs. Bryce sent down in her carriage a large box of ham, chicken, biscuits and butter. She took Mully and two of his friends into town after dress parade to a party at the Clarksons'. When the affair was over it was too late to return to the camp so they spent the night at her house and she sent them back comfortably to camp the next morning in a buggy, in good time for reveille at five-thirty.

The "Hampton and Singleton ladies" of Charleston, remembering that the young men needed refreshment of mind as well as of body, sent down a hamper of books. This was an especially pleasing gift for Mully who was fond of reading. There was time for such relaxation on June 13th, which was a holiday. Mully appreciated the change from the eight or nine hours of daily drill.

He and the rest of the young soldiers considered Mrs. George Howe, wife of a Professor at the Presbyterian Theological Seminary at Columbia, their guardian angel. She sent them delicacies from time to time, offered to have their laundry done, and made them havelocks to protect their heads and shoulders. She worried when one of "her boys" got his feet wet, and would wrap a blanket around him and make him swallow a spoonful of very pungent extract of ginger to ward off a cold.

In spite of all this "spoiling", the young soldiers were anxious to be in action. Mully was elated when the call to arms finally came on Wednesday, June 26th. The Legion was to proceed to Virginia by detachments, the two companies from Charleston constituting the first one. They were to furnish their own uniforms, but the Confederate Government was liable for all other expenses. They marched from camp to Columbia along a heavy, sandy road.

Thoughtful Mrs. Howe was at the station with enough provisions to last through the ensuing railroad journey. She described the farewell in a letter to the mother of Charles Hutson, Mully's companion.[vii][1]

"On Wednesday I witnessed an imposing and affecting scene. Four companies of Hampton Legion were leaving for Virginia. They marched in from their camp, about four miles out of the city, and arrived here about eight o'clock. They rested and refreshed themselves in the shade on the street just back of Mrs. Hampton's garden, affording the opportunity to friends to bid them farewell and invoke the Divine Blessing upon them."

The trip to Virginia was disagreeable because of the heat, dust and crowding, but Mrs. Howe's thoughtfulness had at least saved the Legion from hunger. Mully, accustomed to the flat lands around Charleston, was delighted with the mountain scenery of North Carolina. Almost forty-eight hours after bidding Mrs. Howe good-bye at the Charlotte railroad station in Columbia, Mully and his companions arrived in Petersburg, Virginia.

The Legion was detained here for twelve hours on account of some hitch in the transportation arrangements. They rested all day in a delightful spot outside of the town. Mully seized this opportunity to use the "housewife" (sewing-kit) presented to him by Mrs. Howe, training his fingers to the unaccustomed task of catching up loose stitches here and there. Around noon, the legionaries were given an excellent dinner-probably their last good meal for some time to come.

---

[1] Camp material is taken almost entirely from the Hutson correspondence, as shown in the (bibliography).

Friday night they left Petersburg, reaching Richmond quite late. There they slept on a factory floor finding it comfortable after camp and crowded trains. Saturday, June 29th, they were marched to the Fair Grounds, about two miles from town and set to work pitching their tents. The whole South Carolina military force now consisted of Hampton's Legion, the Davis Guards from Greenville, the Gist Riflemen from Anderson, and the Washington Artillery-all under the command of Lieutenant-Colonel Johnson.

By now there was real fighting at both ends of the Confederate lines in Northwestern Virginia and down on the Peninsula. Everyone felt that a big battle was on the way. Most of the important railroads and turnpikes of Northern Virginia, leading down to the Shenandoah Valley or up to Washington converged on Manassas.

Great was the excitement of the Legion when they entrained on Friday night, July 19th, for Manassas Junction! Mully realized that before long he would be in the thick of the battle, for the dispatches said that fighting had already begun at Bull Run. But the journey was slow and tedious and it was Sunday morning before they reached their destination, less than a hundred miles away.

Logan had just started to eat breakfast when he heard booming of artillery in the direction of Bull Run. Immediately orders came to hasten to the field. The Legion soon began their first march into real battle. Mully was astonished that he could already see the Northern army advancing in a dense column which seemed to fill the whole face of the earth. He could note their progress by the gleam of the bayonets, the roll of drums and the rattle of artillery. The land was so hilly that Mully and his companions hoped the other side would not be able to realize the immense disparity between their large forces and the smaller army of the Confederacy. Had they judged this difference the Union troops might have advanced more confidently and ended the battle then and there.

After being marched and countermarched for some time almost within reach of the enemy's missiles, the Legion was thrown, by order of General Bee, to the left of a corps of flying artillery under shelter of a fence.[viii]

Logan could hear the enemy's bullets whizzing by his ears but he and the rest of the South Carolinians took aim deliberately and bravely stood fire. Soon they were moved to a low place under the protection of a few trees and shrubs. Mully was deafened by the noise and roar of the battle and blinded by the suffocating smoke. It seemed to him almost impossible to tell who was Northern and who was Southern.[ix]

The enemy had captured a Confederate flag and discovered a Confederate signal. One of the Northern officers appeared over the brow of the hill and made the sign. For some time the Legion was deceived, but Logan's quick eye caught the U.S. on his buttons, and dashing at him, seized him by the throat, took away his carbine and sword, made him prisoner. The next moment the line of the enemy appeared on the hill and the real fight began for the South Carolinians. They were thrown back again but never seemed to know when they were defeated. Logan especially remained calm in the face of the most extreme danger.

The Confederates all through the battle were in a dangerous position-pressed hard in the center and at the flanks. The Northern Commander, McDowell, showed masterful strategy in planning his envelopment attack, but the Southerners had a leader even more clever, Thomas Jonathan Jackson. His immovable strength during this battle gained him the name by which he will always be known-Stonewall Jackson.

He was most skillful in hand to hand fighting. He would wait until the enemy was almost upon his own forces and then use the bayonet. His tactics proved successful at Bull Run. The enemy was routed and before they could gather new strength, fresh troops arrived by railroad to reinforce the Confederates. Thus the battle ended in a complete victory for the Southerners.

The Carolinians did their part in gaining the victory. Davis and Beauregard came to the wounded Hampton's tent after the battle and thanked him for the help given by his legion. Beauregard smiled and said: "Your men were really three times beaten but did not and would not know it."[x]

Although danger had only made Logan calmer, the results of this first victory caused him to shudder. His naturally tender heart revolted at the sight of so many dead and dying on the field of battle.

Soon after the Battle of Manassas, early in August, 1861, the Legion was encamped near Broad Run, Virginia. Nearly three hundred of the men were under the care of a surgeon, but Mully was well and kept busy taking care of his friends.

On the sixteenth of August the Legion took up its march to a new camp site in the Occequan [sic] region at Bacon's Race Church. The Northerners were not more than seven miles away. Early's Brigade was expected to join the Hampton Legion and they looked for some close skirmishes. Mully and his camp mates never knew what the next day would bring, and were learning never to look ahead. The weather was rainy and dreary; everyone seemed heartily sick of the hardships, the wretched camp fare, the sticky red clay and, above all, the enforced idleness. Mully had always been particular about his food, careful about his appearance, hating dirt, detesting idleness. But from Marcus Aurelius and Epictetus he had learned how to control himself.

At this time his friend and camp mate, Hutson, wrote about him:

"Our friend, Muldrup, the Dane, has the true blood of the resolute Vikings in his veins: the aristocracy of will is marked in his countenance. He has impressed the men very much and will certainly be our Captain."

On August 22nd, the camp was moved closer to the Occequan [sic], somewhere near the Potomac. It was like being in a wilderness. The South Carolinians had no idea where they were-how far from Manassas, in what direction was Alexandria. The days passed in a monotony of rain and gloom. Mully's friends had one thing to discuss that interested them. Would Lieutenant Lowndes be made Captain, or would it be their own Mully Logan? In a few days they had their wish-Mully was appointed Captain.[xvii]

The effects of war had produced a different Mully only too ready to do his part, but fighting another battle within himself, trying to reconcile the futile destruction of war with his instinct for order and constructiveness.

In adapting himself to these new conditions of life, a compensating quality grew within him. As if to make up for the inevitable folly and waste, he cultivated a gentle amiability. During long days of fighting and privation his associates declared that he treated superior and subordinates alike-with deference and consideration. And yet with himself he was stern and demanding.

By this time the Legion had received orders to be ready to move with light provisions and arms at a moment's notice. They were on tenterhooks-action at last! Anything would be better than this eternal waiting, sloshing around in the mud. They learned with relief that a battle had been fought between the advance Southern columns and the Northerners near Fairfax Court House. Might that mean action for the Legion at last? The news came also that General Longstreet, now at Falls' Church (only about fifteen miles from Washington) had received orders to hold every inch of ground until reinforcement arrived. Wouldn't the South Carolinians be the right men to aid Longstreet?

Mully wondered: "Will we get into the thick of it and even march on to Washington, mud or no mud?"

At last on August 31st the Legion was told to move their camp to a sunny and more elevated spot, near the old site but freer from mud. They were to stay there indefinitely in order to build and guard a battery at Ship Point about ten miles away. The new location was about sixteen miles from Mount

Vernon, twenty-four from Alexandria, thirty-two from Washington.

Continual dampness and poor were now causing much sickness. Many in camp were stricken with jaundice. Logan, never very strong, succumbed to a low fever. He improved when the September sun began to shine, though that same welcome sun made drilling intensely disagreeable, because of the heat.

On the twenty-second of September the Legion decamped and marched about ten miles along the "Telegraph" road leading from Alexandria to Fredericksburg. In the evening they camped on a knob concealed from the Potomac by still higher hills covered with woods. This location was just opposite Freestone Point, near which was a good landing. Close by ran a little creek making for the river through a valley. Mully had only to step to the untented side of the hill to have a fine view of the Potomac. When the men first saw the river they cried out, "The Potomac! The Potomac!" which reminded Logan of Xenophon's description of the exultation which the Ten thousand exhibited at their first glimpse of the sea.

The very next day there was a call to arms. Thirty rounds of ammunition were served to the men and they were marched by a circuitous route of some three or four miles to the rear of a piece of woods skirting the Potomac. The men confidently expected a brush with the enemy; but were only intended to be kept close at hand in case an attempt was made by the Yankees to land in force, in which event their detail of men working at the battery would be endangered. They were ordered to prepare to bivouac in the woods; but late in the evening all of them, with the exception of one company, were marched back to the encampment.

On Wednesday morning, September 25th, the battery of the Legion opened fire. This was returned several times but not with vigor, and without ensuing casualties. The soldiers were kept in motion all Wednesday and Thursday in anticipation of attempts on the part of the enemy to land and get in the rear of the battery. Wednesday night they bivouacked on the slope of a hill a few hundred yards from the battery point, but the enemy could not be decoyed into landing.

On the 14th of October the Legion heard the Evansport battery open fire. The cannonading was heavy for a short time, but soon ceased. A courier arrived stating that there had been much fighting at Fairfax with five thousand Yankee casualties and perhaps one tenth that loss among the Confederates.

Logan heard much talk about moving camp, but this change did not take place until later, and then only temporarily. At one o'clock on October 28th they were marched away from camp with arms, accoutrements and blankets, fully expecting to venture into the enemy's country and tempt them into battle. They marched eight or nine miles, crossing the ford at Wolf Run Shoal. The water was icy cold and the stones sharp and slippery, but they managed to get across. They bivouacked that night in Fairfax County, the Northern Brigade being stationed at Pohick Church. From here pickets could distinctly hear the Yankees' drums. In the morning the men were early astir expecting to go into action, when a courier arrived from General Holmes, commanding this division, with a message ordering Colonel Hampton to return as speedily as possible, as he might be needed in the neighborhood of Fredericksburg.

The Legion was thrown into confusion, nobody knowing what the next move would be, or whether there would be any move at all for months to come. Mully's hopes for taking part in any stirring scenes were shattered.

The autumn wore on into winter and on Sunday, December 1st, the Legion infantry and artillery, followed by the Nineteenth Georgia and a North Carolina regiment, under the command of Colonel Hampton, marched some twelve or thirteen miles to Woodlawns, two miles below Occequan [sic] and five miles above Freestone Point.

Cold weather now kept the camp in comparative quiet, and Logan had time to return his study of the law-Blackstone and Greenleaf. He was still a boy, slender, with straight angular shoulders; his short straggling beard caused his friends to urge him to shave. But he was conscious of his youth and jestingly responded, "No, that would never do. General Lee would never make me a General if I should shave!"[xii]

But on the twenty-eighth of January, 1862, there was no opportunity for study. Logan and his men were roused and ordered to arms, as firing was heard in the direction of Colchester. It turned out that the Texan scouts had had a skirmish with some Yankee cavalry and driven them back. They went to bed and in the morning learned the particulars.

It seemed that these Texans, six in number, were asleep in an old house in Colchester, two Virginians being with them, when enemy cavalry, numbering some eighty or ninety, rode up and rapping at the door, called out: "Come down you damned rebels and surrender!" One of the Texans who was by this time awake called out that they would defend themselves, adding: "Come on, boys! Hampton will soon be here." Lying down on the floor to load their pieces, they fired repeated volleys upon the Yankees. The Yankees fired three volleys and then rode off, carrying with them two of their comrades, who were hit and supposed to be killed. They also left three of their men on the ground, two dead outright and one dying. One of the Texans was slightly wounded.

On the fifteenth of February snow fell from morning until night. A scouting party went out on the road to Pohick Church, including Colonel Hampton, Major Conner, Major Lee, Captain Logan, Lieutenant Hamilton, the Texan scouts, and eight men from each of the infantry companies, making in all about forty or fifty men. The Colonel selected a snowy day because the Yankees would not expect them and, as they seldom stirred themselves on such occasions, there seemed some chance of effecting a surprise. The Northerners that morning had evidently been at Lewis Chapel, situated at the intersection of several roads about halfway between Colchester and Pohick (George Washington's) Church, for their tracks could be seen on the snow. The scouting party continued its cold march until it crossed Pohick Run where it was possible to ascertain that a regiment of the enemy was at the Church, about half a mile from the Run. The group of Southerners was, of course, too small to make an attack. In spite of their small number, however, the Colonel would have placed them in ambush and given the Yankees a surprise had it not been so late. As it was, the day was drawing to a close and the men returned to camp.

By now the winter was melting into spring. On the twenty-fifth of March the Legion was encamped near Fredericksburg, Virginia, where it stayed until the next month.

During the morning of the seventh of April, 1862, the battalion assembled in formation, and the order was read communicating the tidings of Beauregard's victory in the West and the sad loss sustained by the Confederacy in the death of Sidney Johnston. At three o'clock on the morning of the eighth orders came to prepare to move. Whiting announced that General Johnston had commanded him to march the Legion immediately against the enemy. Logan and his camp mates were under the impression that they would cross the Rappahannock and move in the direction of Stafford Court House. But on reaching Fredericksburg, to their surprise, they were marched away to the southward. They began their line of march on the rainy morning of the eighth of April, travelling roads slippery with the same sticky red clay, which made Mully shudder, for the roadside ditches seemed to run with blood.

At night when they bivouacked, the wagons containing their blanket were far in the rear, the ground saturated by the unceasing rain, their garments wet through to the skin, and a few hard biscuits carried in their haversacks constituted their only food.

With the coming of summer and Logan's arrival near Richmond the young Captain had more than his wish for "stirring scenes." At the bloody battle of

Gaines' Mill, July 7th, 1862, he was wounded for the first time—sustaining a bad foot injury. In spite of this painful hurt he insisted on going in an ambulance to command his company at Second Manassas, on August 29th.[xiii]

At this time his father and sisters lived in Columbia, South Carolina, in a little cottage on the corner of what was then the Arsenal and Blanding Street, and it was here that the four Logan brothers came home on furloughs in the summer of 1862. Colonel George was the eldest, then came Dr. Sam, Daniel, and Mully, who was treated by all as a wounded hero, because he was on crutches. Dan and Mully were always together and looked like twins. When Dan's own Crescent Rifles of Louisiana were disbanded, because of heavy losses in the field, he joined Mully's command. He preferred being a private near his Captain brother to having an officer's rank as Aide-de-camp, and the friends who nursed Daniel Logan in his last hours, December 1st, 1862, spoke of the way he uttered "Brother" with such yearning accent that no one could realize how much that brother Mully was to him.[xiv]

But after that summer furlough there were no more reunions under the cottage roof. Instead there were many weeks of anxious suspense, for the brothers were soon scattered far and wide. The Doctor and Captain were in Virginia and Brother Joe in Mississippi.

The eldest brother, George William, was having a very exciting career in Mississippi. As Lieutenant Colonel of the Chalmette regiment he participated in the defense of forts on the Mississippi river below New Orleans, protecting that city against the Northern fleet under Farragut.

Mully's regiment was now attached to Hood's Texas Brigade. In September, 1862, he was made a Major (over two senior officers) for special gallantry in the field. After the Sharpsburg campaign his regiment was transferred to Jenkins' South Carolina Brigade and Major Logan was advanced to the rank of Lieutenant Colonel and as such, served in the Suffolk and Blackwater campaigns.[xv]

Chapter III

War and Love
1863-1865

The third year of the war, 1863, was an especially eventful one for Logan, for it was then that he met his future wife. On Easter of that year he was traveling from Petersburg to Richmond, a distance of only twenty odd miles, but consuming several hours because troops were being transported.

As the dusty car was crowded Logan had to stand, leaning on the back of a seat, weary and pale, trying to steady himself against the jerking of the train. Sitting near him with a party of friends was a dainty girl in a fluffy lavender dress-very different from the drab homespun of wartime. Under her beribboned poke bonnet her grey-blue eyes sparkled as she talked animatedly with her companions. Logan watched her with a feeling of home-sickness for his sisters in South Carolina. How lovely she was, and what a contrast she seemed to the grim confusion of his army life-the mud, the squalor, the blood and agony!

She opened a lunch box and began to take out fried chicken, biscuits, and little iced cookies. Suddenly she looked at Logan, her eyes softening sympathetically at the sight of his tired, pale face. She leaned toward him and his heart beat high. But a young man, evidently a relative, intervened. After some discussion the young relative left the girl's side and approached Logan with a glass of ice water which was almost as welcome as the luncheon would have been. Evidently they had decided that he might be insulted at being offered anything so prosaic as food. Mully confessed long afterward that he overheard the cousin say: "No, if he were a soldier I would, but officers put on too many airs."

He did not see his lovely fellow-traveller (sic)why? again for some time and soon had almost forgotten the incident. But in September he was back in Petersburg again. One day after dress parade General Jenkins asked him if he would like to be presented to some young ladies sitting nearby in their carriage. In spite of his shyness, Logan assented. The introductions were made and he heard the name of Miss Cox. Then one of the group leaned forward from the back seat of the carriage.

"Colonel Logan, I have seen you before, though you may not recall the occasion."

The rays of the setting sun were in Logan's eyes, so he found it hard to distinguish her features, but he thought he recognized the voice. He bowed and smiled when Kate Virginia Cox reminded him of the Easter train ride. So here was that lovely girl again!

He soon obtained her consent to call that evening. After that he went to the house where she was visiting almost every day as long as she was in town.

General Jenkins accompanied him frequently on calls and embarrassed the bashful Mully one evening by saying in front of Kate: "Now look at that modest young man! You should see him on the battlefield; he is dashing and gallant-completely transformed. Oh, I wish you could see him in battle, though of course that would be no place for a lovely young lady!"

Kate smiled as Mully blushed and fidgeted under General Jenkins' compliments. Somehow she seemed to guess all kinds of things about Mully's family and his life in Charleston.

"How did you know about her?" he asked one day, when she mentioned his eldest sister, Elizabeth, by name.

"I nursed your college friend, Major William Brawley, at my house for a month when he was first wounded. He told me all about you, but," she blushed, "he said he hope you and I would never meet. I wonder why."

Mully was flattered by this last remark but a little jealous at the thought of Kate spending so much time with his friend. (See "My Confederate Girlhood")

He saw her later when she was visiting the Jones family near Petersburg, and it was very hard for him to say goodbye when the Longstreet corps was ordered to Tennessee. He felt that he might never again have a chance to meet that spirited girl with the sparkling grey-blue eyes.

He was too shy to attempt a correspondence, but remembering Kate's devotion to flowers, kept a keen eye out for horticultural specimens, mailing Miss Cox newspapers from time to time with pressed blossoms between the pages. He did not put his name on the packages, addressing them in his execrable handwriting. Kate told him afterwards she had no idea where the papers had come from.

During the autumn of 1863 she saw from the Richmond papers that Colonel Logan was acting commander of sharpshooters and skirmishers for General Longstreet, at Chattanooga and Knoxville. She read that in the fighting around Chattanooga he was in immediate command of all skirmishers from Hood's division. She was particularly interested in the description of his skill and gallantry, in the pursuit of the enemy from Loudon to Knoxville, where on two occasions he charged and routed them.[xvi]

The newspapers also stated that on another occasion, near the end of October, Longstreet ordered Hood's Division to cross Lookout Mountain, proceed up the road in Will's Valley, and feel out the enemy reported coming in force from Stevenson. Crossing the railroad leading to Chattanooga was another road which, if left unprotected, would enable the enemy to cross the Tennessee River, and intercept the division. To guard against such an emergency, Lieutenant Colonel Logan, with fourteen companies of Infantry, was ordered to hold the place at all hazards. This was at midnight in a strange country, and against overwhelming odds. But for Logan's courage and skill the whole of Hood's division would have been surrounded and crushed.[xvii] Anyway, this was Kate's biased opinion.

In March, 1864, Logan had a leave of absence and almost immediately rode out to Clover Hill where Kate Cox lived. He was welcomed by her little brother, Willie. Kate had gone for a walk. Mully paced up and down waiting impatiently on the front porch. Soon Kate came up, rosy from her walk in the bracing spring air. Her ruffled white grenadine dress, so fresh and charming, should have made him ashamed of his shabby army outfit; but he forgot all else in delight at her warm welcome. Her grey eyes were more sparkling than ever.

Before she could say a word, the front door opened and a fine looking man with dignified bearing and keen grey eyes appeared on the verandah. He had neither beard nor mustache, but his graying hair fluffed out on his head and came down in front of his ears in sideburns. He wore a stiff shirt and collar open several inches at the neck. Across the opening was a black bow tie. He had on a long tailed woolen coat over trousers of the same dark material. He was Kate's father, Judge James H. Cox.

"Welcome to Cloverhill," the words boomed out in the resonant voice of an orator. This voice suited very well his fine presence, for Judge Cox had been for many years presiding magistrate of Chesterfield County, representing his constituency for a number of terms in the General Assembly, being at one time Speaker of the House. He also represented his County in the Constitutional Convention of 1849-1850 and

1861. He was now in charge of his Clover Hill coal mines.

The Judge proceeded at once to invite Mully most cordially to spend his month's leave of absence at Clover Hill. The month passed in a blissful dream for the young people. Their most eloquent silences were while he held skeins of wool for her to wind, for Kate was always knitting for the soldiers.

Judge Cox, though he admired Mully's quiet ways and brilliant qualities, was unwilling for the young people to be formally engaged until their world should be more settled. But there was an "understanding" by the time Colonel Logan left, and they were even permitted to correspond-quite a concession for those days. They were also to be nearer to each other than they had been except during leave, for Mully's command of mounted infantry had now come to join the army of Northern Virginia.[xviii]

From May 12th to 16th of 1864 Logan was in the battle of Drury's Bluff.[2] He was assigned to the duty of inspecting and reorganizing the picket lines from north of Petersburg to the south of Richmond. He accompanied Beauregard in moving headquarters from the lines north of Petersburg.

After the promotion of Colonel Gary, Logan became a full Colonel in command of the regiment which had been the Hampton Legion, which was soon to see hard fighting. Mully's comrades said that he showed great bravery under showers of bullets and bomb shells. During one of the advances upon Richmond on the north side of the James, several of

---

[2] Also known as Drewry's Bluff. Ed.

the other officers dodged down and held themselves close to the backs of their horses, but Colonel Logan sat erect in the saddle as if on dress parade, smiling at the uneasiness of the others.

On May 16th when General Grant crossed the Chickahominy, Colonel Logan was detached with his regiment and the Twenty-fourth Virginia Cavalry to delay the Federal advance until the head of General Lee's column could cross White Oak Swamp and take a position between Grant's column and Richmond. At this time Logan requested Lieutenant Albergatti in charge of the picket to take a ride with him. Though Albergatti expected the directions, of course, to be along the line of the Confederate pickets and videttes, Logan led in the direction of the Yankee line flanking a Federal vidette until they drew up in full view of the Federal picket post and stopped only when the enemy had mounted their horses in pursuit. Colonel Logan had deliberately estimated in mind the risk and the distance back to safety and remarked to his comrade, "Now we will have a horse race!" The race was run safely, but under a shower of bullets.

At the Battle of Riddle's Shop, June 13th, 1864,[xix] Logan's horse was shot in the chest. The animal was in panic from pain and fright. Logan dismounted, saw that the horse was not killed and was in the act of remounting, when a bullet struck him, entering one shoulder and coming out the other without touching the spinal column. He succeeded in remounting but his arms were paralyzed and he could not control the horse. A companion caught the bridle and assisted Logan to an ambulance. He was taken to the rear badly hurt for the second time during the war. When he met the infantry column filing across the fields to cover the road to Richmond, he had the satisfaction of knowing that he had really accomplished his purpose, for the advance had been delayed enough for the first division of General Lee's column to take its stand, protecting Richmond from Grant's army.

Logan had been in extreme danger a score of times, yet he seemed to bear a charmed life so far as death or capture were concerned. Never once was he to see the inside of a Northern prison. This time he was taken to Mrs. James Dunlop's home in Richmond for treatment and care. As he was very ill, he knew it would be a long time before he could return to his command, so he was beside himself with eagerness to convalesce sufficiently for the transfer to the Cox home, Clover Hill-a drive of twenty miles. He longed for a sample of Kate's nursing!

When he arrived at Clover Hill several weeks later he was not disappointed. The morning after his arrival she brought his breakfast into the library, where he lay on the sofa fully dressed in his shabby grey uniform. In contrast, how fresh and lovely Kate looked in her new lavender sprigged muslin, her dark hair parted in the middle and curling rebelliously in spite of Mammy's attempts to make it look demure.

"Why do you do this?" he protested. "I'm well enough now to go to the dining room."

"Not down those crooked dark basement stairs!"

"But I can't eat before you do."

"Oh, I had my breakfast long ago."

"Did you do all this for your other South Carolina patient, Brawley?" he asked.

"Yes, and he preferred bacon to ham just as I am sure you will. We think bacon should be used only in the quarters. That taste shows you're not a Virginian."

"And never will be?" he asked slyly.

Kate blushed.

When he seemed about to start teasing again she threatened: "If you don't behave, I'll send you to father's South Carolina hospital at Grasslands. You'll have to sleep in a tent and there'll be no Mother and Ben and Mammy to spoil you. Wouldn't you miss that?"

"Perhaps I'd miss something else even more." Then after a pause, "Maybe I'd miss this wonderful coffee."

"But Father has that same kind at Grasslands. He stored away sacks and sacks of Government Java before the war. He's stingy with us at home, because he likes to keep it for his spoiled soldier patients."

"Well, spoiled or not, we're lucky. This is the first real coffee I've had for years. Do you know what they're asking for it in the Oriental Restaurant in Richmond?[xx] Three dollars a cup, and a dollar and a half for one order of bread and butter to go with it. For coffee's sake, will you promise not to send me away-not even to Grasslands?"

"Well, maybe not just yet. I was there myself the other day and all those South Carolina soldiers were talking about you."

"What did they say—something uncomplimentary?"

"I won't answer that question, but I met your brother Dr. Sam while I was there. I think he liked me."

"I think he must have! What did you wear?"

"Oh, we wear what we can these days. Fortunately, Mother has always kept yard lengths on hand. Susan is a marvelous seamstress but she loves her handiwork and hates my habit of wearing best for every day. We play a regular game of hide and seek. If Mammy were not on my side, I'd never put on a dress that wasn't three years old."

"Susan's present effort looks about three hours old!"

She laughed merrily. "We found it in the linen closet, packed in among the sheets. Mammy has charge of the sheets, you know!"

The Clover Hill darkies all took Mully to their hearts. If Mammy, Susan, and Sarah, Polly, Uncle Ben and Uncle Alfred had not liked him, Kate would have been in a quandary! For she always appreciated her Clover Hill people's love and approval. She couldn't love any one not approved by them.

The weeks passed by, all too rapidly for Mully, for though he was suffering physically, he was blissfully happy in Kate's company. When he was better, they drove along the country roads, chaperoned by the Cox's old coachman, Uncle Alfred. The landeau had a plum-colored lining, and Uncle Alfred, sitting high on his coachman's box, wore a plum-colored coat to match. All Mully and Kate could see of him was the gleaming silver buttons on the tail of his coat, for the sympathetic old darkey showed them only a discreet back. Had he disliked Mully, his back would have been eloquent of disapproval.

During Mully's convalescence he read long hours with Kate. Plutarchs' Lives was a favorite of both and

Mully loved to talk about what constituted greatness in men. Of course, they admired most of all the Southern hero, General Lee. Once embarked on this subject Mully was inclined to orate:[xxi]

"We have in Lee a rare combination—," he began one afternoon on the front verandah.

Kate was struck by the fervor of his voice. She looked at him with pride, but said banteringly, "Prose, my dear sir, is inadequate. Pray express yourself in nobler terms."

Not to be daunted Mully readily replied:

"A combination and a form indeed,

Where every god did seem to set his seal,

To give the world assurance of a man."

She clasped her hands approvingly.

"But seriously," went on Mully, "Lee has the highest order of genius, as valorous as Alexander; as brilliantly talented as Caesar; as stern in his virtue as Cato. He has the genius of Napoleon-the unselfish patriotism of Washington," his voice died away in awed respect.

Kate's eyes filled with tears, for Lee was her hero, too.

"I suppose you know he had a wonderful mother?" she suggested. "I have a great uncle who thinks women don't have much influence, even on their own sons, and he believes Father is outrageous to encourage my reading and study."

Logan's face flamed with indignation. "I'd say that it's not your father who is outrageous but your uncle. The development of women's mentality will elevate womanly qualities, just as increased intelligence produces higher and purer phases of morals and religion. No matter who wins the war, after all this devastation, we'll have to build up a new country and we can't do this without our women. The more you read history, the more you will find that great advances in human progress have been generally accompanied, if not caused, by social changes elevating the position of women."[xxii]

How Kate loved him to talk that way! If there had been any doubt in her mind about it before, she knew now that she loved Mully.

About three months after he was wounded, Mully was well enough to leave Clover Hill. He commanded his regiment throughout the fall in the many skirmishes along the left flank of the Confederate lines.

In the autumn of 1864 the Federals were on the Nine Mile Road trying to advance on Richmond. His friends said Colonel Logan showed remarkable coolness and skill, saving the Legion from massacre. The Hampton Legion had been ordered into line of battle on the Charles City road and there remained until relieved by the Georgia Infantry on the right. The South Carolinians moved to the left until the Williamsburg road was reached and then deployed to the right, defending that road. A few minutes steady firing halted in confusion a line of the enemy which had emerged from a body of woods some three hundred yards in front. These were white troops and evidently new recruits. At this juncture the Legion was ordered hurriedly to the Nine Mile Road down which were coming an overwhelming horde of colored Northern troops. It was now evidently the object of the Southern General in command to have the head of the line continue until it reached the road, where a battery of artillery and a squadron of mounted men were in position. He appeared excited and urged on his men.

The enemy had got within forty yards of the low breastworks along which the Confederates were racing, when Colonel Logan suddenly realized that before he could reach the desired position at the road he would be overpowered. In defiance of the commands of his superior officers he decided to halt his men and commence firing. The first volley staggered the advancing line and the second put them to flight in front. Their overlapping line swept around the Confederate flank capturing the artillery, but Logan seized the battle flag of the Legion and, leading his men, charged to the rear and whipped and drove away the enemy, recapturing the artillery and securing hundreds of prisoners. His poise defeated an overpowering enemy and, his men later said, no doubt saved Richmond again.

In December, 1864, General M.C. Butler[xxiii] was made Major General and he applied for the appointment of Colonel Logan as Brigadier General to command Butler's Brigade. Although one of the junior colonels from his state, and only twenty-four, Colonel Logan was commissioned on February 15th, 1865, Brigadier General of Cavalry, the youngest man of that rank in the Confederate Army.[xxiv] He was ordered to join General Johnston in North Carolina.[xxv]

At parting his regiment presented him with a horse "as a mark of their confidence and esteem." He named the horse Virgie after his sweetheart and her state. He went to Clover Hill to say goodbye before he left Virginia. How proud Kate must have been when she saw the slim figure in grey with his General's sword, belt and hat, his boyish face aglow with joy at seeing her and pride in his promotion. But in spite of surface optimism, there hovered in the back of his mind a foreboding that the South was defeated. He was determined to do his best until the bitter end, but he knew already that he was fighting for a lost cause.

He tried his best to express this to Kate as they sat together in the cozy library at Clover Hill before a bright coal fire listening to the February sleet trickling against the small window panes. Nothing could dampen Kate's enthusiasm.

"We will win-General Lee will join General Johnston when he comes from North Carolina!"

But Mully sadly shook his head. He could no longer shut his eyes to the fact that the Confederacy was doomed. There was no use trying to explain this to Kate because Clover Hill, with its coal mines, still prospered. But the far South especially was down to the bone. Only that morning he had received a letter from home depicting the suffering in South Carolina. Sherman was already on the march there, burning and pillaging the little which remained. Perhaps at the very moment the Northern General was entering

Columbia where Mully's father and sisters were in refuge. He shuddered.

Kate's sympathetic heart was touched by his piteous expression. "Please, please don't look so sad. Everything is bound to turn out right. Think how brave our soldiers are!"

"Yes, brave a thousand times," he said. "No matter what happens our soldiers are not to blame. No men ever fought better. As years pass by, the deeds of the Confederate soldier will be valued at their real worth. [xxvi] But bravery is not all. Our soldiers are starving and ragged. On my way here I stopped at the crossroads store. The shelves were empty, of course, but because this is a coal mining district, the stove glowed hot. Huddling close to the fire were several of our men. They seemed to be trying to store up heat before venturing out in their miserable rags. But they were only storing up chilblains[3] on their poor feet covered with carpet in place of shoes."

"Oh, why didn't you send them here? Father is always glad to do what he can."

"Thanks, dear, but even your father can't feed and clothe a whole army. With adequate material and supplies the South might have held her own indefinitely. She is worn down by want-not subdued by arms."

Listening to his words from which all hope had fled, Kate for the first time came face to face with defeat. Silent tears were coursing down her cheeks. In Mully's sympathy for her he forgot his own despair. He tenderly laid his hand on her arm. "Kate, I was

---

3 A skin ulcer caused by exposure to cold or moisture.-Ed.

wrong when I spoke so hopelessly. We want a little less despondency and a little more effort."

"But what can we do, especially if the Yankees win?"

"We can help build up again what was torn down by the war. We have our life together and we are young. Our country is also young and by everybody doing his little part to build up the force of public character, some day we shall have on this continent a great nation inhabited by a great people. Are you going to help?"

"Oh, yes, I promise." And they clung together like two children lost in a dark tangle of vines which seemed too strong for their hands to tear apart.

The next morning early he rode away to join his command.

In March, 1865, General Logan commanded his brigade in North Carolina. At the battle of Bentonville General Joseph E. Johnston occupied the main road upon which the enemy was advancing, and pressing him in front and rear. He sent General Logan several miles down a road to guard his flank with the promise to withdraw him should there be danger of his being cut off. General Logan held this position for several hours. By then the firing of the flank made him feel that his men were in danger of being cut off from the main army, so he hastily mounted his brigade and ordered them back.[xxvii]

Finally, within a few hundred yards of the point at which he had left General Johnston, he was confronted by a large force of the enemy who opened fire upon the head of his column. What should he do now? Quickly he decided to wheel to the left and leap a fence and a ditch. The brigade followed him through a small detour, crossing an apparently impassable swamp in which the horses were bogged at every step. Then they dashed over the main road at a gallop, between two corps of the enemy moving in opposite directions. A few minutes later the enemy corps met and closed the road behind General Logan and his entire brigade. But for this promptness, and his habit of correctly judging the position of troops by the sound of previous firing, the capture of the brigade would have been inevitable.

But fighting by now was becoming almost a secondary matter. The crux of the situation was the lack of supplies. About this time General Logan received the following letter:

Nelson, N.C.
April 7, 1865

General,

The forage question is growing to be a serious one and unless a prompt movement of the troops to a point within 10 or 15 miles of Rail Road is made, they cannot be furnished a living ration. All corn within 20 miles of this place has been hauled to camp; from this time, unless this disposition of troops is made, as spoken of by us, the round trip by wagon train will be over 110 miles. Our forces have destroyed the Rail Road track for three miles this side of Nahunta Depot, the point agreed upon as our Depot; how far they are ordered to destroy the road I do not know. I now propose Black Creek Depot and am ready to throw supplies there. Please attend to this immediately and inform me by courier of your plans. Should this movement be made, please send this communication to Majors Harding and Williams Q.M., and let them arrange the proposition of transportation to be kept at Camp. I desire them to let me have all the wagons possible on this end as my forage arrangements will cover a large scope of country. All wagon trains now here will report to Camp with their loads on tomorrow evening; from these wagons will be selected the reserve train for Camp purposes. I would be glad if you would order Capt. Green again to report to me tonight for temporary duty; it will be necessary for me to remain here probably several days longer. I have written to Maj. McClellan, A.A.G., on this subject and have urged that a disposition of the troops be made so as to throw the bulk of the horses near our proposed Depot. I would suggest that all serviceable horses be sent to the immediate vicinity of the depot provided the organization can be kept perfect.

Mr. Black, my clerk, has been directed to see you as far as my quarters are concerned.

Allow me again to urge the importance of action in this matter. I will require ten men each from Maj. Harding and Maj. Williams for the purpose of shelling and sacking corn. Let them come with 16 days rations by next wagon train. Please say to Maj. Biggs that I hear of a great quantity of bacon both at little depots along line of Rail Road and through the country.

> I am, General, yours truly,
> George Melton, Major General.

How distracting it was to receive such a letter and to feel there was nothing to do in response!

Logan was now with General Johnston's army and he remained in command of Butler's Brigade until the surrender at Greensboro. He was in charge of the rear guard shortly after the retreat through Raleigh; and near that city General Logan at the head of Keith's battalion made the last cavalry charge of the war.[xxviii] He was with Johnston and Butler on April 18th, 1865, when they met Sherman at Durham's station, North Carolina, and agreed on a tentative treaty after news of Lee's surrender had reached there.[xxiv]

Logan's youthful pink and white face seemed to astonish Sherman who remarked: "You are certainly, judging from your appearance, the youngest General in either army. You are from South Carolina, I hear. I don't know just what I can say in apology for anything that happened there, for after all, as you know, war is war."[xxx]

Logan did not answer. He could not respond affably, for even at that moment he could almost feel his pocket burning with the letters which he received not so long ago from his sisters in Columbia. There Sherman had done his worst!

Chapter IV

Hard Days in South Carolina
1865

By the middle of April, 1865, General Logan could no longer entertain the slightest hope that his family had been spared during the February raid in South Carolina.[xxxi] They had supposed that Sherman would attack the more important city of Charleston, and for that reason had moved to Columbia, feeling sure that they would be safer. But they were mistaken.

On the sixteenth of February, 1865, Columbia was bombarded.[xxxii] Judge Logan was particularly alarmed because the firing was directed toward the arsenal near his home. When the house across the way was struck by a shell, he and his daughters hurriedly packed their valuables in trunks so that they could go to some less dangerous spot. Before they could leave another shell fell in the adjoining yard and the family retreated to the basement. The bombardment ceased at four o'clock in the afternoon and the family decided to remain.

Early the next morning, February 17th, Sherman entered with his army. On they came, marching past in endless columns. In great contrast to the gaunt and ragged Confederate soldiers whom the Logans had seen from time to time, these men in blue looked well fed and clothed; and somehow, in spite of yesterday's bombardment, Mully's sisters felt no real fear as they looked at those blue coats. Their father, meanwhile, had procured a Northern guard who condescended to take tea with them. The younger sisters gazed at the newcomer as if he had been some curious animal. They eyed his uniform distrustfully. When he left, little Seppie seized the chair he had sat in and dusted each part of it, then set it off by itself.

Some while after tea there was a cry of "Fire!" The girls rushed out of doors and saw the sky illumined in two or three directions. "What's the matter, what's the matter?" they asked the guard, who stood stiffly at the front door.

He looked at them calmly. "The soldiers will soon put the fires out," he answered. "You'd better go quietly upstairs. After such a hard day perhaps you'd better try to get some sleep."

The girls did go upstairs to their rooms-not to undress but rather to pile one dress on top of another, making themselves into walking wardrobes. By this time fires were springing up on all sides-another, another and then another. The family hurried into the dining-room and put spoons and forks into their many layers of pockets. Each time they looked from the windows the skies were brighter.

Soldiers were rushing into the streets in groups of three and four, shouting and yelling. Some had poles with burning cotton on their tips. Others were kicking around lighted balls of inflammable material. The family servants had wrapped up their treasures and rushed away, all except one faithful slave, David, the butler. He got a ladder and tried to reach the roof of the house to extinguish the fire by laying down blankets soaked in water. Twice he tried, but the yard had filled with soldiers and they pulled him down each time.

As the night was cold Lizzie took a blanket from one of the beds and pinned it around her father, who had suffered a recent illness. A soldier quickly plucked it off and disappeared with it. She got a second and another man said, "Let me see this old rebel," and off that blanket was snatched. A third attempt met the same fate.

The men in blue now swarmed into the house, bursting open the store-room door and beginning to plunder.

The girls went into the basement and, hauling out four trunks, stood by these in the yard. Lizzie's large one was surrounded by soldiers, and one, saying, "Let's see what's in here," drove his axe into its side. As the contents rolled out there was a scramble. The sisters clustered around their father and hauled the smaller trunks away to the center of the yard.

"Your house is on fire," several soldiers had called out from time to time, but the sisters hoped this was only an ill-timed joke. When the raiders streamed out of the house the family knew that it was actually on fire. They hurried through the gate and hastened down the street toward the country, not knowing where to go except to get as far as possible from that fearful scene.

The younger children, Seppie and Georgie, began to cry bitterly, but each held on to her little trunk, dragging it by the side straps. The soldiers jostled and pushed and one stopped and laughingly called, "What are you crying for, little girl? See we've built a big fire to keep you warm."

There was one kind Infantry officer whose heart was touched. He and a Cavalry officer joined the family and Judge Logan thankfully accepted their offers of help and begged their escort. One trunk went up on the horse's back and the other two were dragged by the girls and the friendly Infantry officer. The Cavalryman was a Lieutenant Lamar. "Where shall we take you?" he asked.

The Judge thought for a moment. "To the lunatic asylum!" he directed.

The officers looked at him in astonishment. To their unspoken question Judge Logan explained that the place was well built and out of range of the heavy firing on the city.

The Logans, sheltered at last, breathed more freely. Lieutenant Lamar, after the location of the Logan cottage was described to him, said he would go and see what he could save. He came back in about an hour to tell them that house was too far gone in flames for him to venture in, but brought a bolt of sheeting and gave it to Lily, whose fresh young face seemed to arouse his sympathy.

Saturday, Sunday and Monday Judge Logan and his four daughters spent in the private apartments of Dr. Parker, superintendent of the asylum. These were days of anxiety and nights of terror. Fires were burning in all directions and the yelling and shouting of the soldiers added their discord to the more distant crashing of the bombs.

The Logans were hungry but could get nothing to eat, for Dr. Parker could feed only the invalids and very young children. Their hunger was doubly trying as they had to serve others with cups of milk and slices of bread. They spent four nights sleeping on the carpet in Dr. Parker's parlor with numerous other refugees, all thankful to have a spot to rest their heads.

On Monday Sherman marched away from Columbia, his band sounding the notes of Yankee Doodle. The raiders bore away every horse, cow and mule; every carriage and wagon.

A few houses in the vicinity of the General's headquarters escaped burning. One of the homes still standing belongs to Mrs. Bryce, a friend of Mully's. She insisted that Judge Logan bring his five daughters to her home, and there they remained three weeks. Friends in Greenville, South Carolina, and Augusta, Georgia, sent the family food and clothing. Dr. Chisholm invited them to his Charleston home, later lending them his house in Columbia, where they stayed for several months.

Meanwhile the brothers had sent their army horses to Columbia. This gave the Judge an idea for making a little money. He and his son, Samuel, started a stage line, consisting of an open spring wagon filled with wooden chairs, drawn by two horses, driven by themselves. They transported passengers between Branchville and Columbia, as the Railroad there had been completely demolished. The Judge supported his family in his way until they moved back to Charleston.

The struggle of that summer, 1865, is described in the following letter from Mully's sister Lily:

Columbia, September 3rd, 1865.

My precious brother:

It is a very long time since we have heard from you or Kate, but I hope from your silence that you are both well. We are all getting on extremely well for these dreadful times, but we have a great deal to do. Papa still drives his cart as a means of making a livelihood and Brother Sam is busied preparing for his winter lectures and attending to his practice here, which consists, unfortunately, of mostly "no pay patients." The Coffins find it very difficult to get on and the family (both sexes) work very hard. The boys drive teams and keep a store, but have been extremely unfortunate. Even has lost two fine mules, his principal support, and George and Grange have had their store robbed. These are really dark times for many, my dear brother, and we are more blessed than the majority of our friends. I can never feel grateful enough for the kind Providence that has raised us from so many threatened evils. The very house we now occupy was an unexpected luxury. It belongs to a Major Hill who is now north. He objected to hiring it out for fear of its suffering abuse, and begged his friends to recommend some one who would take care of it for him. Papa was mentioned and we are now comfortably settled in a home "for nothing," which is more luxuriously furnished than many houses which bring five thousand dollars a year without trouble. We are here until January, then our destination is uncertain, but my opinion is that eventually we will return to Charleston. Brother Sam leaves next month for that place, and will endeavor to get an office of some kind for Papa. As for himself, most persons believe that the Med. Col. will obtain quite a large winter class, and we hope he may realize a little there. I presume, dearest Bro., that ere this you have rece'd one of my many letters informing you of the loss of your mules and other possessions. For fear of the contrary, I must repeat that your two horses, Carrie and the other, are all that were saved. There is some dim hope recovering your trunk, but nothing positive. The servants have all gone, but Tom and Cornelius, whom we hire. Mr. Bunch was here some two months ago. After making a fruitless endeavor to recover some of your losses, he left for Charleston. Our spirits and health are excellent.

Yours, Lily.

This joins up with a letter from Mully's father written the next February in which he says, "I will not deny that I could use some money-for we are rather short of the comforts of life, but for God's sake do not go in debt for it! I would rather wear homespun and see the girls in it too than wear clothing, sleep on a bed, or sit at a table that was purchased by borrowed money!"

These were indeed hard days for South Carolina. The State had lost her credit and everything else that had given her prestige and power. She could obtain nothing without cash, and cash she did not have. South Carolinians thought that Lincoln's aim had not been the freedom of the slaves so much as the preservation of the Union. His proclamation was a "war measure" and had he lived no doubt he would have conciliated the Southern States. His assassination by J. Wilkes Booth set the radicals free and gave up the South to destruction.

The Reconstruction Acts were passed. Never was South Carolina to forget the horde of Carpet Baggers who arrived with the new law. They were so named because when they came they brought their all in small carpet bags, but it took many trunks to carry away their loot. The natives who worked with them were called Scalawags, which means a stench in the nostrils. Controlled by such people, the negroes, inexperienced and ignorant, voted as they were directed. They were made to believe that if ever the former Confederates won control they would be re-enslaved. This made it seem that every negro Democrat was an enemy of his race. According to South Carolina opinion, the darkies themselves were getting nothing; the Carpet Baggers everything.[xxxiii]

A favorite plan of the radicals was to organize mobs of strikers who would travel to the rice fields on the rivers and use threats to compel the workers to quit, even when they were quite satisfied with their wages. A gentleman farmer, Henry de S. Elliott, had an experience with one of these mobs. The organizers gained control of his workmen and drove him into the plantation store house. Elliott had the reputation of being a good shot, so the strikers kept out of range, besieging him for about a week. At last one of his party got through the lines. He reported the matter in Charleston and troops were sent at once to his relief.

The Carpet Baggers continued to create race antagonism. The older darkies seldom responded but the younger fell for threats and promises. Long before the election of 1876, there was a baseball riot. A game was advertised between a Charleston nine and one from Savannah. Influenced by Carpet Baggers the negroes threatened to interfere. Mully's relatives and friends were already playing on the Citadel Green when the negroes began to mob the visiting team. Fortunately, U.S. troops came up and required the negroes to take one sidewalk, the whites the other. Troops marched between, thus separating the two factions. There was much shouting from side to side, but in this order the Georgians were escorted to their steamer without further molestation.

There were countless other incidents to prove that politicians and Carpet Baggers felt far more animosity toward the South than the officers or even the rank and file of the Union Army.

Meanwhile in Virginia conditions were far better than in South Carolina.

Chapter V

Virginia
1865-1867

After the surrender of Johnston's army in North Carolina, General Logan's one idea was to reach Virginia as soon as possible. He mounted his fleet mare, Virgie, and on the last day of his journey covered the then stupendous distance of sixty-five miles. Not even the trial of such a journey could divert Mully's mind from his intense anxiety. Clover Hill must, he was certain, have been directly in the path of that last sad march.

He pictured a desolate Kate standing by the smoking ruins of their home. Or, worse still, suppose it had happened in the night and Kate-! No, he must not think of such a possibility!

On the way he met Colonel Venable, one of General Lee's staff, returning slowly after the surrender. Eagerly Mully asked him, "What of Petersburg and that part of the country? Have you recently seen any one from Clover Hill?"

"Not since April third, General. On that morning our army was on the march through Chesterfield when Orman Latrobe, a member of Longstreet's staff, recalled that we were only a mile from Clover Hill. He rode in to see Judge Cox who then sent a messenger to Lee and Longstreet, asking them both to midday dinner. Of course, we were expected to come along, too."[xxxiv]

"And Miss Kate, did you see her when you got to the house, Colonel?"

"Of course, Sir, but she had eyes only for General Lee. They were speaking earnestly together but I could not catch the words. From her expression I knew she was trying to comfort and hearten him. When the butler came in with juleps General Lee refused to take one. This seemed to make a great impression on Miss Kate."

"And where did she sit at table?" Mully was trying to picture Kate as she must have been on that day.

Colonel Venable smiled. "By General Lee, of course, although I didn't notice that she ate anything. Her mother wanted her to help Longstreet and cut up his food, but Lee refused to let her go. General, that was a delicious dinner!"

But Mully's face clouded. "How about the Coxes now?" he insisted. "Are they still at Clover Hill or was the place burned down?"

Venable could tell him nothing more.

At dusk Logan finally reached Clover Hill.[xxxv] He and Virgie went slowly down the long lane, savoring the joy of seeing everything standing as he had left it, the picturesque house with its rambling wings, dormers and gables, and its wistaria-covered [sic] porch. His happiness was too much to bear and he rode even more slowly as he approached the house, his eyes misty with excitement.

He came to the hitching rack, dismounted and tied his horse. As he started up the steps Kate ran to meet him.

"Oh, I knew you were safe! I knew you would come back, no matter what they said."

The front door opened and there was a swishing of silk skirts and the scent of lavender. Mrs. Cox approached and stood as close to her daughter as her hoop skirt of dull black would allow.

"Welcome, welcome," she greeted Mully, her eyes full of happy tears.

Suddenly there appeared from nowhere the old darkey, Uncle Ben. Without a word he took hold of the mare's bridle to lead her away to the stable.

Mully and Kate soon wandered out into the box-bordered garden with its twilit scent of hyacinths, calycanthus and daffodils. They avoided as far as possible the mention of the recent sad days, planning happily for their wedding in May. It seemed only a moment before the big bell sounded and they were called to supper in the basement dining room.

Even after the privations of camp life Mully paid little attention to Mrs. Cox's homemade delicacies. How could he think of food with Kate's lovely grey eyes looking into his and her sweet voice ringing in his ears?

By the light of the rustic candles he could barely see the faces of Judge and Mrs. Cox at the far ends of the table. Everything seemed subdued-almost as dim as the outlines of the massive sideboard, the paraffin lamp long unfilled during these past days of blockade. Would the South have to remain always in this atmosphere of dimness and scarcity? Was there nothing he could do about it?

Then through the shadows as the head of the table he heard Judge Cox's resonant voice: "Well, well, young man, we feared you were never to sit amongst us again. Just yesterday some Northern soldiers came to the coal mines with the only newspapers we had seen in a long time. There was an account of the surrender to Sherman in North Carolina. You should have seen us all, especially Kate, poring over the list of commanding officers looking for your name."

Here Mrs. Cox broke in. "Could I be blamed for thinking that you had been taken prisoner, wounded, or killed?"

"Oh, Mrs. Cox, I'm so sorry that there wasn't some way I could have saved you all that needless worry!" Then turning to Kate, Mully asked, "And what did you think?"

"Oh, I just couldn't believe that anything had really happened to you! I shut myself in my room as if that would shut out fear, and it did-it did. When I came down to supper last night I wasn't a bit gloomy like the rest of the family. And now they're wrong and I'm right."

"Yes, I'm thankful for my good fortune," said Mully. "My brother Sam did not fare as well. He sent on all his possessions in a wagon drawn by four mules in charge of a man who later absconded with the entire load. This was a bitter blow to my family, as they had already lost so much by the Columbia disaster. But why should I talk so gloomily? In spite of sorrow we are feeling at the loss of all our hopes we should try to make this a joyous reunion."

The Judge looked solemn. He could not refrain from saying, "I am very much disappointed that Kate is marrying under these circumstances. I had always expected to give her a fine, big wedding."

This sort of talk did not hurt Mully's feeling, for he knew the Judge's sincere affection for him and realized that only the unsettled times were at fault.

Soon the conversation lapsed into pleasant plans for the marriage. The next morning very early Kate and her mother went to Richmond to buy what they could from the meagre stocks in the stores.

That afternoon, Judge Cox and Mully sat on the veranda making plans for the future. "I understand from Kate that you want to be an attorney. I was wondering if that would interfere with a proposition I had in mind. It's hard for me to make the trip back and forth day after day. Would it be possible for you to take over a part of the work superintending the mines?"

"Oh, Sir, I hardly know how to thank you for such an opportunity. By the way, I've always wanted to know the history of the Clover Hill coal mines. Could you tell me more about them, Sir?"

"Our deposit of coal was discovered in 1837, Old Uncle Moses came in one day with a large sack of coal which he brought to my father exclaiming, 'Master, look what I found in dat gully down dar!'"

"Father was deeply impressed, for he knew this meant there was really coal on the place. He later helped me arouse the interest of business men in Petersburg and Richmond and to raise enough to sink a shaft and really start work on the basin. For the coal was discovered on my share of the place."

"By January, 1840, my brother Joe and I had chartered the Clover Hill Company. The method of getting the coal to market was at first by wagon to Richmond and from there it could be transported down the James River to the ocean. The business grew apace, and coal from our mines found a market as far North as Boston. You see it was excellent for the production of illuminating gas. This is a good selling point although bad for us here, for the presence of so much gas causes frequent explosions."

"Who worked the mines at first?" asked Mully, "Your negroes?"

"Yes, but they were not experienced enough to do it alone. We also brought over miners from different parts of England, especially from Wales." He paused.

"What about the Clover Hill Railroad, Sir?" Mully asked eagerly, for railroads were one of his favorite subjects.

"I was coming to that. The railroad company was chartered the year after the mines-1841. This corporation was authorized to build a railroad from our pits to join the Richmond and Petersburg railroad, a distance of eighteen miles. The incorporators were all Richmond capitalists except Moncure Robinson, who was from Philadelphia and interested in building railroads in Virginia."

"But, Judge, how did you ever keep the mines open during the war when there was no Northern market?"

"Because our mines were among the principal sources of coal for the Confederacy." The Judge paused and regarded the young officer intently. "Well, how do you feel now about helping us out?" he finally asked. "Your advance salary can start on Monday."

"Of course I'd be glad to have anything I can do. A young lawyer is seldom overburdened with work, is he?"

Judge Cox smiled. "How much law have you studied? I understand you entered the war just after you graduated from college."

"Oh, but I've been reading it every spare moment during the last four years, Sir. I intend to work hard all summer with my law books. In the fall I'll be ready to apply for a license to practice."

"I shall be glad to help you in any way I can, especially with the railroad work. It's a bargain," and rising, Judge Cox gave Mully a mighty handshake.

After the uncertainties of war, it was a great relief to the young man to realize his affairs were shaping up so satisfactorily. He had only one twenty-dollar gold piece in the world; he had carried it all through the war. With money coming in regularly he would be free from grinding financial worry. Already he found himself thinking ahead to further projects involving not only his own tiny world but the whole devastated South.

There was the sound of gravel crunching on the path followed by the entrance of the ladies, and the rest of the afternoon was given over to describing and displaying Kate's trousseau. Mully felt he needed a trousseau, too, so with his first salary he bought himself the best suit he could find, which wasn't very good. No one expected at that time to see well-tailored clothes.

They were married at Clover Hill on the twenty-fifth of May. Kate's much loved pastor, Mr. Tizzard, officiated. The South Carolina Logans could not come, of course, but standing near the bride were Kate's four brothers, Henry, Piper, Johnny and Willie.

"If only he were there with the rest!" Kate whispered to Mully just after the ceremony. He knew to whom she referred-her favorite brother, Edwin, who had died of camp typhoid early in the war. From Edwin, Kate had gained her love of reading, especially of poetry.

Some of the Cox cousins had come to the wedding, the beautiful Molly Grymes and Kate's two aunts, Mrs. Woolridge and Mrs. Mann from Woodlawn. Both aunts were already encouraging Kate in her love for housekeeping and fine old china and furniture, just as her mother had developed her interest in gardening and the Judge in reading.

Mrs. Walke and her doctor husband of Physic Hill arrived for the reception. The medico looked disapprovingly at the table piled high with Mrs. Cox's delicacies. All through the war he had struggled to hold his lavish-handed wife down to the simplest food. Now the scarcity habit was so ingrained that he could hardly realize the war was over. It had been a secret only to him that during his pre-prandial naps, Mrs. Walke had feasted her wartime guests Chinese fashion with sweets served first. By the time the ascetic doctor had reached the dining table, Mrs. Walke and her co-conspirators were ready to start from scratch with soup. The servants also enjoyed the gentle joke on their doctor. The presence of the delightful Walkes helped break the tension at the wedding. Everyone had tried to be lively, but sad memories of absent faces and of those lost on the battlefield cast their shadows also on the hard days still to come.

After their wedding Kate and Mully remained for a while at Clover Hill. In 1886 (sic)[4] they moved to a house overlooking the James River at Tenth and Decatur Streets in Manchester, now South Richmond. This colonial-style, square, white clapboard home was designed by the architect, Alfred Rives, who had every opportunity to understand beauty, for he was born and brought up at lovely Castle Hill in Albemarle County, and had lived abroad. His father, William C. Rives, was twice Minister to France.

When the busy General could come home early in the afternoon the young Logans drove around in a neat little carriage behind a handsome pair of horses. Kate loved showing her husband this part of Virginia which was new to him, but with which she was so familiar.

One thing to which Kate was unaccustomed was hiring help. How could it have been otherwise when the servants at Clover Hill had just been a part of the place? One day a likely looking young colored girl came to the Decatur Street address, looking for a job.

"What are your qualifications?" asked Kate.

When the applicant seemed puzzled, the question was repeated in a more specific form: "What can you do? Can you wash?"

---

[4] This is a typo, the Logans moved in 1868—Ed.

Good manners alone kept the girl from snorting with disdain.

"No, Ma'am, I's a fancy servant. I ain't never 'meaned myself to washing,'" adding with contempt, "Mandy done our washin'."

Kate apologized: "Perhaps you can cook-oh fancy cooking, of course, like" —hopefully— "desserts or—or salads, maybe."

"No, Ma'am, I ain't no kitchen hand. I's a educated pusson."

"A lady's maid then? You understand about hairdressing or-fancy sewing?"

This time the girl only looked discouraged. Kate was becoming discouraged too. "Well, then, what did you do?"

The girl brightened up at this direct question: "Who, me? I had plenty to do, Ma'am. I used to hunt for Ole Miss' 'specs.'"

In the spring of 1866 a baby was born to Kate and Mully. He was christened Joseph Edwin, but lived only a few months. He was succeeded the next year by Anna D'Oyley who soon followed her brother to the grave.

This double sorrow did not make Mully lose his sympathy for others. He spent much time investigating Manchester conditions requiring relief. When he found out how many people needed aid, he sent a circular letter to leading citizens asking them to a meeting late in December, 1867. Thus was formed the Manchester Board of Relief with General Logan as founder and President.

About this time he was also made President of a spur of the Richmond and Petersburg Railroad from

Chester to Osborne's on the James River. This Port Walthall branch, run for the benefit of the Clover Hill Mines, was a spur in more senses that one for General Logan. His new work intensified Mully's interest in railroads, an interest which was later to affect his entire career. Already he realized the immense importance of developing railroads as a means of building up a country.

Chapter VI

Family Life
1868-1872

I n May, 1868, the Logans were made happy by the arrival of a daughter, named for her mother, Kate Virginia. At this time Mully's two sisters, Lily and Georgie, were staying at his house and they made a great pet of the baby.

The home was increasing in beauty, for Kate loved flowers and she and her mother worked together making terraces down to the River and setting out old-fashioned plants from Clover Hill. Mrs. Cox had a magic hand with flowers and could make anything grow. Mully was almost as interested as the women and he often told how his great-great-grandmother, Martha Daniell, had written her "garden kalendar" in Charleston to remind her neighbors just when to do their planting. He would sit on an iron bench with his papers on a rustic table before him, while he looked around at the spring lawn with its foamy mists and banks of snow drops beneath sweet almonds and

Japanese quinces. He loved the smell of calycanthus and mock orange, mixed with perfumes from narcissi and jonquils. Later in the spring he teased Mrs. Cox about old plants, saying he knew only moss-roses and could never tell which were damask and which were musk.

He declared that she only pretended to know their names because no one could contradict her. He was especially interested in York and Lancaster striped pink and white roses.

Mully's happiness would have been almost too great to bear except that keeping pace with his joys were burdens heavy for his still slender shoulders. His law practice was growing rapidly and the work at the mines was very harassing because explosions were frequent.

On March 8th, 1869, when he came home in the evening he found Kate waiting with a letter in her hand from her brother Piper. Mully entered the comfortable sitting room with its lovely old mahogany from Clover Hill. Kate ran for his slippers, then seated him in a large chair in front of the fire.

"Read it, read," she begged. Kate's quick mind always ran ahead and Mully could hardly keep up with her, for his reactions were slower. To humor her he did not bother with the inscription at the top of the letter but began at once:

"I am sorry to communicate in this note bad news."

At the words "bad news" Kate seized his hand. "Oh, go on, go on," she interrupted. "I know someone is ill!" She was apt to fluctuate between the heights of joy and the depths of apprehension.

Mully's patience was inexhaustible. Imperturbably he continued to read: "In the first place this morning Hall's Pit was discovered to be on fire. And one of the dams recently made has given way."

Kate interrupted again, this time in relief. "Oh, the bad news doesn't concern the family but the mines!"

"This is bad enough." He continued reading the letter to himself. When he had finished he said, "There's trouble in the Bright Hope Mine too and your brother says they need me. I can't wait for supper here, for I must start at once for Clover Hill." This was twenty miles from Manchester.

When Mully reached the mines the fire was almost extinguished. Repairs were made within the next few days.

One morning when Mully came to Clover Hill Mrs. Cox met him at the door. She was tremulous with anxiety, "Oh, Mully, what shall I do? The Judge has broken his leg! I always feel helpless since the death of his brother the doctor."

Mully forgot the coal mines for a moment. Dr. Walke was summoned and Judge Cox was made as comfortable as possible on the parlor sofa. In spite of his suffering, he chose this time to talk over various matters with his son-in-law, who was generally too busy to stop and discuss matters at length.

"I'm sorry, my son," the Judge began, "to burden you further when your law practice and the coal mines need all your attention-especially now when I must give you my work to do also. But yesterday I came across a pamphlet of mine written in 1843 and it started my mind to working." He paused, "I may be asking too much."

"Please continue," urged Mully, for he knew the Judge's ideas were always interesting and constructive. "What was the subject of your pamphlet?"

"The school system of Virginia. That sounds somewhat ambitious doesn't it? But I should like to awaken your interest in this subject right now. Virginia needs your clear head and boundless energy to arouse general discussion of her schools, so neglected during the war years. And there's another thing to mention along these same lines. I see almost daily discussions in the paper about various Northern plans for the negro's education. Have you made up your mind on this very controversial subject; that is, whether or not a freed-man should be educated and to what extent?"

Mully's face was alight with interest. This was a topic to which he had already given much thought. "I'm so glad you brought that up, Sir, as I can express to you ideas which I fear to give voice to among my younger, more hot-headed acquaintances. You know how I dislike acrimonious discussions. My belief is this:[xxxvi] The freed man is now a citizen and even self-interest should prompt the whites to prepare him for greater usefulness. As a laborer, ignorance is his greatest deficiency; this would soonest be removed by the school system. As the race advances, education of the negro can be changed to suit his advanced condition."

"Splendid!" applauded the Judge. "It is the Bible case of the little leaven leavening the lump. I knew before asking you that I could have your interest and cooperation."

"If I might make a rather personal remark," Mully ventured, "I certainly do admire the breadth of your thinking in contrast to that of many of your contemporaries. I hear that during the Secession Convention you were not at all on the side of war and yet you gave your sons among the first."

Judge Cox sighed. Perhaps he was thinking of his son Edwin, dead of camp typhoid so soon after the fighting started. "Well, that is finished now, but I did do all I could in my small way to ward off war. I knew it was an unequal fight, to be followed by almost certain disaster and defeat. We could expect no allies and we had neither army nor navy. I saw no possible chance of success.[xxxvii]

In addition I felt strongly that we should wait until Lincoln had committed some overt act of enmity which would justify us before the world in our secession from the Union. Only after Lincoln had called for the seventy-five thousand troops to quell the rebellion did I feel I could sign the ordinance of secession. And then after the war, if Lincoln had lived, everything would have been better. When I read your sad letters from South Carolina-but it is too late to go into all that now."

In 1870 frisky little Katy was delighted to welcome a brother named for Mully and the apple of his father's eye. The General loved family life and was finding it increasingly disagreeable to spend so much time on the road between the Manchester home, the law and coal offices in Richmond, and the mines, twenty miles away. So he decided to move to Richmond.

It was hard for Kate to leave the home on which she had spent so much love and care. A new home was bought on Seventh Street between Leigh and Marshall in Richmond. From there the family moved to Leigh Street between Seventh and Eighth, near the Valentine studio, at the northeast corner of Capitol and Ninth Streets.

The artist, Edward Valentine, took a great fancy to little Katy's bustling ways. To her great delight she was allowed to dabble in his modeling clay. She was as intense and important about this as her father was in moulding his work and career.

The General was trying to work up his ideas for helping Richmond to resume her old place as an important capital. All the furies seemed let loose on Richmond during this year of 1870. In April the floor of the Capitol collapsed, causing great excitement. The feeling was that no public building was safe. On October 1st the James River washed away Mayo's Bridge and many houses and factories nearby. Oddly enough, the rest of the city was made too dry, for the water works were put out of commission by the flood. Also, Richmond was left in darkness, for every one now was becoming accustomed to gas lights and the necessary fire in the gas works was extinguished by rising waters. It would seem as if visitation by water were enough for one year, but this period of calamity had also its crown of fire. On Christmas morning the historic Spottswood House was burned down. President Davis, Generals Lee and Grant had all been housed there at different times. Only eight persons lost their lives in this conflagration, but the psychic effect was bad, recalling, as it did, the Evacuation and burning of Richmond five years before.

Mully had been in North Carolina at the time, but Richmonders had often described to him the terrifying confusion of the night of April 3rd, 1865, when the Northerners entered their city. Strangely enough, it was the Southerners themselves who started the fire. By an act of the Confederate Congress orders had been given to burn all tobacco and cotton so that these products would not fall into the hands of the invading Federals. Plundering mobs also helped to spread the flames[xxxviii] and the dawn of April 4th saw huge conflagrations. Still more oddly, it was the invaders who finally extinguished the fire.

On April 10th, 1872 Mully received a letter from the Richmond Enquirer. "Read it, read it quickly," Kate said with her usual impulsive curiosity.

He hastily looked over the note. "Oh, it's nothing," he announced with assumed indifference. "Only Mr. Kirby at the request of the board of directors of his paper is asking me for editorials on various subjects."

"What will your first subject be?" asked Kate.

"But, my dear, I've only just read the letter. I can't decide as quickly as this."

"But I can! Listen! What brought you up from your old home, South Carolina, to Virginia? Where did you and I first see each other? What are you President of now, and what is most of your law work about?"

"Oh, you're saying it in your funny puzzling way, but I know what you mean. I'll make my first editorial on railroads."

Chapter VII

Railroads and the Panic
of the Seventies
1872-1874

M ully's first article for the Enquirer was entitled: "Railroads, the Arteries and Veins of the Body Politic."[xxxix] Kate read it by herself with all eagerness.

"We regard it as a good sign," she read "that in the depressed condition of business in the South, the railroad interest seems to be the most active and progressive one at present. And the fact that this is due to Northern capital is by no means a discouraging feature."

Mr. Kirby, the editor, was evidently pleased with the subject. Cranks had recently been writing to the paper about the folly of having any railroads at all. How much better, they wrote, it was to do as their Grandfathers had— "depend entirely on the noble horse." Kate always sniffed at such outmoded ideas.

"Why not oxen, then?" she would ask. "Or still better, Shank's Mare?" She continued reading:

"It is folly then to be constantly deploring that these great roads will be controlled by Northern capital. This will not of course build up our country if we do not help ourselves, but it will furnish us the opportunity to do so, and only ordinary business enterprise and energy will be necessary to insure us the benefits. It will also open new and large markets for our manufacturers and we should prepare to take advantage of this by building up our factories."

"When the General writes like this how can anyone disagree with him?" was Kate's fond thought. She was getting more and more into the habit now of speaking and thinking of Mully as "The General."

In June of this year a second boy was born to the Logans and christened James Henry for his grandfather Cox. Four-year old Katy was delighted, as that meant somebody else to manage in her bustling way. Little Muldrup had prayed for a brother but was puzzled at the supineness of his new playmate. Judge Cox pretended to be offended at his attitude.

The new happiness was soon clouded by the death of Mrs. Cox in August. It again threw extra work on Mully at the coal mines, for the Judge could think only of his own loss. There were more and more explosions in 1873 and Mully had to do a good deal of squashing around in the mud, after water had been used to put out the flames. He was infected with typhoid-pneumonia, which was long in passing.

Before he was well Kate had him propped up in the four-poster, writing a short article to the Enquirer, signed "Citizen," and called "Our Muddy Water." He wanted to prevent as far as possible further illnesses like his own. This was followed shortly (August 30th, 1873) by a leader on the same subject. This last Editorial suggested the Kirkwood (St. Louis) method of filtration and ended categorically: "Let us have clear water in Richmond. It can be done, and it should be done and done promptly."

But there were more serious things than the water supply to write about this autumn. For the panic of the seventies was by now well under way. On November 21st he sent to the Enquirer an article which almost might have been written during the 1930's.

"Number of our mechanics and laborers are idle, and these, the most productive class of our community, are consumers but no longer producers. Under such circumstances we are becoming poorer every day and it behooves us to consider seriously what can be done. There is no reason why so many workmen in this city should continue unemployed and so much legitimate business remain paralyzed. Some relief can be afforded, and it should be given. The banks should lend to all that bring good securities quickly, freely and readily."

The next spring a new baby, Martha, was born to the Logans. But like her eldest brother and sister, she lived for a few months only.

Mully adored his family, but domestic griefs could not be allowed to interfere with his work for his wife, his living children and his state. Echoes of his personal sorrow are dimly heard through these words of courage in one of his Editorials in the Manchester Courier for September 5th, 1874:

"If you faint in the hour of adversity, your strength is small . . . The people of the South have suffered so long from the despotic rule of a corrupt and absolute party that there prevails a disposition to regard our Republican government as a failure. This is truly the 'recklessness of despair' to which it is weakness to yield. We want a little less despondency and a little more effort."

On an autumn evening in this same year of 1873, Mully and Kate were seated in the library. The wind was howling without. But within there was a bright coal fire in the large open grate. Gas in the chandelier above shone in fanlike flames, and oil lamps also cast a cheerful glow. How delighted everybody was to have kerosene back again! Kate loved to watch the flickering flames bring out the highlights on her polished mahogany. Lovely furniture was like the breath of life to her, while books were Mully's favorites. The two had combined their loves in the high desk bookcase with its fluted columns. This sturdy but graceful piece stood against the wall just across from the windows opening into the garden. The lower pair of bookcase doors were veneered with an intricate patter of waves and swirls. The children called the lower cubbyhole a "house." Here were kept Mully's magazines and newspapers on the topics of the day. In one corner were his own clipping book and speeches in pamphlet form. These were all arranged chronologically in his methodical style. When Mully wanted to use the middle part as a desk, all he had to do was to open back the slanted crossways door, then pull out two side supports. Presto, change! The door rested easily on the supports and became a convenient writing slab. Inside were many mysterious pigeonholes. Each was neatly labeled, "Bills," "Letters," etc., but as Kate used the desk most of the time and have very little sense of order, the labels really meant nothing, and bills were apt to be under letters and letters under bills.

The desk part was now closed. Mully stopped in front of the upper doors and peered through the tantalizing latticed glass, murmuring to himself the names of some of his favorite books. He gazed affectionately at the flaming rows of Bohn's Standard Library in editions of 1855 and later. Among other books there he found Schlegel's Lectures on Modern History. In contrasting colors but on the same shelf were Lamartine's History of the French Revolution and many other translations into English. But Mully liked best to read French in the original. He now swung open of the doors and gave pats of recognition to his Rousseau, Sainte-Beuve and Taine.

History and biography occupied the largest space on the shelves with a growing autographed library of Memoirs by General Logan's former companions in battle. Science also had a prominent place. Among other books on this shelf were those of Darwin and Spencer. There were essays galore, including recent ones by Walter Bagehot and John Stuart Mill on "Liberty" and "On the Subjection of Woman." Woman's rights and education were subjects dear to Mully's heart.

There were also open shelves at both ends of the room. On one of these were Mully's books on elocution. A favorite was a large marbled volume called, "Modern British Eloquence," published by Harper and Brothers in 1852. Mully was always practicing oration, for he realized how close and personal was the spoken word.

Kate was beginning to grow jealous of his interest in books. She pulled him away from the case and seated him in his easy chair beside the table, while she herself sat on her favorite stool at his feet. "Come on, General. I don't care for all those poky writers. When you hobnob with your books, you don't seem to belong to me."

"Remember, my dear," he chided in answer, "It's not clothes, after all, but books that really make the man."

Kate smiled. "Well, let's have something from my made man then. Why don't you read me more of that New South article of yours? You're always telling me I'm extravagant—let's have the part beginning 'Economy'."

"But I've read that before."

"It doesn't matter."

Already he had reached over and picked up the note book. Then he began to read:

"Economy is one of the first requisites of prosperity: but there is a great difference between the economy of an industrious and frugal population and that comparative non-consumption of an unemployed population which is caused by a depressed production . . ."

"Read me some more," Kate demanded. She looked very demure with her soft hair in braids twisted around her head in a coronet. She was wearing a dove-grey cashmere dress with buttons down the front, diagonal folds of the cashmere crossing at the waist. Each fold was ruffled on both sides. A V-shaped, rose-point collar was pinned together at her throat with a cameo. From a black velvet ribbon hung a large open locket. On one side of it was a miniature of little Muldrup and on the other, one his golden curls.

Mully looked at her admiringly, then continued his reading:

"As the depressing influences which no man cited, fully account for the present paralysis of the body politic, health will be restored when those causes of disease are removed; and the existing prostration of business thus indicates no inherent defects in our social economy, but only temporary derangements."

"Why don't we have a kind of government-boss to correct these derangements?" asked Kate. "I'd suggest you, only you're too gentle. We need somebody who's a regular hard-mouth tyrant like the overseers the Northern writers used to put into their books about the South."

Mully looked at her in astonishment. "I wish my mind worked as quickly as yours! You've given me just the subject I want for my next Editorial."

A few days later[xl] the article appeared, and Kate on seeing it, decided she would never have recognized the thought as her own. She read it in part:

"The apprehended danger of Caesarism—that is, a reckless disregard of constitutional limitations tending to the establishment of a centralized absolutism in the place of a Federal Republic, and thereby increasing influence and power of the executive department of the government, is a subdivision of the system of popular government which must in the end be fatal to Republican institutions."

"What does all that mean?" Kate teased her husband.

"Why, simply that your hard-mouthed overseer will not do for this country. We don't want even a gentle overseer."

"Like you?"

"Not even like me. You see, we're individualists here. We don't want apron strings to keep away self-development and spoil the force of public character.[xli] Even a benevolent despotism would make us like children overtrained and overindulged. Such a child forgets how to think for himself and loses ambition and initiative. Self-government is the central idea of America's being. To vindicate the sovereignty of her people is her first responsibility."[xlii]

"Well, what is the remedy then?" Kate asked. "You say we mustn't have a dictator and the banks must help, but how?"

"First of all, we must seek for the deep underlying causes. I have it all written down in this 'New South' article. Shall I read you some more of that?"

"Of course."

Seated as usual in his arm chair, with Kate at his feet, he began to read:

"In seeking to account for the present prostration of the country, we must not only become familiar with phenomena, but we must also know the special conditions under which they appear.

In addition to the waste of wealth caused by the war, there is also a loss of production caused by the transition from a state of war to one of peace. This means a sudden and violent change from vast expenditures to rigid economy. At the close of a war the demand for materials and supplies is curtailed. While the capital and labor engaged in their production are seeking other employment, a large number of soldiers who had been unproductive consumers are also discharged, and the labor market is overstocked. The decreased consumption depresses production precisely at a time when it must be increased before this surplus labor can find employment. Activity of business caused by forced or extravagant consumption during war, or during a period of speculation following it, is not real prosperity, although production may be unnaturally stimulated until the bubble bursts. By having in mind this distinction, we can always discriminate between real and fictitious prosperity."

"I like that idea," Kate remarked judicially. "But didn't you work on it a little too hard? Can't you make it simpler for the paper? I would."

"But, my dear, I am I and you are you! You can write as fast as you talk and talk as fast as you think—or faster! I have to deliberate."

He continued to read: "The transition from war to peace deranges production. Excessive consumption during war reduces stocks, and until they are replenished, production is stimulated; but when the deficiency is supplied the extra demand ceases, and as soon as the era of speculation which usually follows war is passed, depression results before capital and labor can readjust themselves to a peace basis. The trying period of readjustment must be passed before prosperity can be restored.

"The large indebtedness of the country tends also to depress production, because the whole of the national debt represents that much available capital not only lost and destroyed without an equivalent in wealth, but which has been also withdrawn from circulation. This capital would otherwise be employed in production.

[xliii]"No doubt there periodic conditions of depression are due in great measure to the improvements in machinery, and in the means of production. Temporarily, before new kinds of production are developed, a large part of the country's labor is without employment.

[xliv]"The present prosperity of France has been compared in this connection with the prostration of the United States, and it might well be argued that something must be wrong, if the industries of the country cannot stand the tests of wars and of financial panics. No system of industry can be regarded as substantial if it is unable to bear these extraordinary trials, which are inevitable in all countries. Any old hulk may ride a smooth sea, but only the sound ship will survive a storm."

"But how shall we bring the ship into harbor? The remedy, the remedy, where is that?" Kate insisted.

"I was just coming to that." Patiently he took up his interrupted reading.

"In seeking a remedy we should first inquire how confidence is to be restored, and here properly belongs the consideration of the currency question."

"Oh, at last!" Kate sighed with relief.

[xlv]"The volume of the currency cannot be arbitrarily fixed in amount in a large and rapidly growing country without soon becoming vastly inadequate to the wants of business as the medium of exchange, and affecting injuriously the trade and prosperity of the

country. This reacts against the credit of government, and loss of confidence will probably ensue. Such arbitrary restriction therefore will not necessarily bring about specie payment any sooner than an opposite policy. But an adequate supply of currency under some self-regulating plan may so stimulate business and advance the general prosperity as to secure appreciation even sooner than under the restrictive policy. In short, some wise financial policy, based upon sound principles is what is most needed to advance the general prosperity of the country, and this is the common ground upon which both extremes may meet."

"Well, what do you mean by a self-regulating plan?"

Again he explained patiently: "Almost any system that is self-regulating is preferable to one where uncertainty prevails from the apprehension of arbitrary interference. This restriction by law of the volume of the currency, and the absence of all provision for self-adjustment, are the serious defects of our system and they require correction.[xlvi] We are inclined to advocate the "Convertibility scheme!'"

"And what may that be?" she asked.

"What is popularly known as the Interconvertibility Scheme was first prominently introduced to public attention by the late Mr. Greeley in an editorial of the New York Tribune in November, 1871. The bill now before the House of Representatives was introduced by Judge Kelley, of Pennsylvania. It is generally known as the Interconvertibility Bond Bill, and has been for several days under discussion. It provides, substantially, that the holders of United States notes in sums of $50 or some multiple thereof shall, upon presentation as described, receive in exchange therefor an equal amount of bonds, coupon or registered, bearing interest at the rate of 3-65 per centum per annum, payable semi-annually, and that said bonds shall be redeemable on demand by payment to the holders of the principle sum and accrued interest in United States notes.

"Well, it's too much for me!" she said.

Way down Mully probably wasn't sure himself that he knew what the depression was about and how to stop it. But he still had the feeling that Richmond's recovery could best be brought about by making her a railroad center. In the Manchester (Virginia) Courier for September 19th, 1874, he wrote an editorial definitely in favor of "The Railroad Interests of Richmond."

"Richmond," he said, "has no defined railroad policy and the disadvantages she is now laboring under as to her Southern and Southwestern business are largely due to this fact."

After stating the difficulties in full, he suggested the organization of a board to study railroad matters for the further development of the city. Mully's awakening to the importance of railroads was soon to become an obsession.

Chapter VIII

War Memories
1875

The year 1875 was one of mixed blessing and anxieties for the Logans. On June 3rd there was born another baby, Margaret Polk—nicknamed Meta almost from the beginning.

Naturally, Judge Cox was happy, but he was beginning to feel his age and could no longer give of his time and limited strength to the coal mining work. General Logan also was too busy with law work and writing to go daily to Clover Hill. Both mine and railroad were allowed to pass out of the hands of the family. The railroad became at first "Brighthope", the name of one of the mines. Then it was the Farmville and Powhatan, having been extended from Chester to Bermuda Hundred and from Clover Hill to Farmville. [xlvii] Later the name was again changed to Tidewater and Western. The entire railroad was abandoned about 1917.

Beside the Brighthope mine, the other principal pits were named Raccoon and Cox. The Cox, of course, had been the first Clover Hill mine opened. Franklin Stearnes now acquired the coal properties and they afterwards passed to others who opened up the Cox shaft during the coal strike of 1902 and worked them for some years. This was the last extensive mining in the Clover Hill Fields.

General Logan was now more anxious than ever to return home as early as possible to be with Kate and the new baby. On an evening early in the month he would not have hurried home had he known what was in store for him.

As usual he rushed up to Kate's room where found her looking very lovely as she lay propped against pillows, a soft blue scarf draped about her shoulders. "Where is the baby?" he asked.

"Mammy has taken her into the nursery with the other children."

He kissed her on the cheek and started to leave the room, but she laid a detaining hand on his arm. "Oh, no, don't leave yet, I have lots to talk to you about."

"Scolding?" he asked, his eyes twinkling above the sober black he wore these days in an attempt to look older.

"Well, maybe. Father tells me the mines have been sold. So, in future, young man, you won't be able to use your Clover Hill work as an excuse for not going to parties with me," said Kate, who longed to show off her General in the busy society life of Richmond. He loved to have his own house full of company but would not go to other peoples' parties. He was still slight and delicately built, with the soft skin and pink cheeks of his boyhood days. He was growing a beard, as he had done during the periods of the war when shaving material had been hard to procure. "It makes me look older, my dear," he explained when Kate begged him to shave.

"Because you're bashful you needn't think you can hide behind your beard like an ostrich," she chided. "Your beard won't save you this time, nor your talk about being too busy either. You've got to go to Charleston for that meeting late in July. It's given in your honor-isn't it? Well!"

"But what would I talk about?"

"Why should you ask me? You used to pretend to be quiet and silent, but that isn't an excuse any more. Don't you write for the papers almost every day? Don't I have a time getting you to your meals when you are scribbling in your precious notebooks? And how about those charity meetings when you preside? And your work in court?"

"But that's different. Now if all I had to do was write something! But to stand up in that hall and look at all those-those school and army mates whom I haven't laid eyes on for all these years! I'd feel so-so-ashamed."

"You'd feel just the way you should. What have you to be ashamed of? Who, among your classmates has done more than you have since the war? Why are those South Carolinians giving a reception in your honor unless they think you are worthy of it? You remember, General Wade Hampton wrote you once that your name would be of great service in his work for rehabilitating the South. And he's in charge on July twenty-first!"[5]

"Oh, I'd forgotten that other meeting. I suppose I'll have to speak there too!" The General sighed wistfully: "I wish I were more like you or little Kate. You two just love to talk-the more the better."

"You'll have to learn to love it, too. This speech will be the first of a series-just see!"

He groaned and began to finger the heavy watch chain which was draped across from one waistcoat pocket to another.

A large and enthusiastic gathering of the Washington Light Infantry was held at the Charleston Hibernian Hall, 105 Meeting Street, Monday evening, the twenty-sixth of July at eight o'clock. As the members of the Infantry arrived those who had known General Logan before greeted him warmly, the younger members were introduced, and all expressed their satisfaction at seeing him. At nine o'clock the meeting was called to order and the presiding officer, Vice-President Bryan, presented General Logan:

"We have come together tonight to extend a greeting to a friend and comrade. The mere mention of his name to those who have been with him on the fields of Virginia is sufficient. In the words of General Hampton, when he introduced General Logan to the Legion in Columbia lately: 'There is no man more fit

---

[5] Hampton having been elected governor of South Carolina after a contentious election whose outcome had to be decided by the South Carolina Supreme Court.-Ed.

to recount valiant deeds or to illustrate their spirit.' I introduce to you, Gentlemen, our comrade, the ornament of the Washington Light Infantry and of the Hampton Legion, General T. M. Logan."

After this greeting Mully no longer needed Kate's urging. He pushed his notes aside, for words came to him readily in this atmosphere of friendliness and admiration.

"There are occasions," Mully began, "when feeling becomes too deep for utterance and words prove powerless to express the emotions of the heart. Gentlemen, this is my position before you tonight; and I am the more embarrassed because of the flattering terms in which your welcome has been conveyed to me. I thank you sincerely for this reception. It is an honor so marked and gratifying that I am at a loss for language to express suitably my appreciation of it.

"I find myself at the home of my boyhood, among my friends and companions of my youth, after an absence of fourteen years. One would naturally be affected most deeply on such an occasion. But, gentlemen, my feelings are the stronger when reminded that I am being thus welcomed by the illustrious command in which I received my first lessons as a soldier. My sympathies with your association, therefore, are peculiarly strong. Fourteen years ago last January I attached myself to your Company A, which was then in the service of the State; and I remained on duty with that Company, as a private, until the fall of Fort Sumter. During those three months I was taught the drill and discipline of the camp, and I then learned the duties of the soldier and the obligations of the officer. If there was anything of worth therefore in my subsequent military career, much is also due to those personal friends whose partiality gave me the position I held in Company A, of the Hampton Legion Infantry. It was the kindness of those friends, some of whom I now see before me, which placed me in command of that Company.

"Gentlemen, I have watched with peculiar interest that movement on your part, which, originating in 1873 at the celebration of your anniversary, culminated in your recent visit to Bunker Hill. This work has been a glorious one and nothing that you have ever accomplished in peace has been more fruitful of happy results. That movement, gentlemen, received the hearty endorsement of the great State of Virginia whose adopted citizen it is my honor to be, and you may rely on her cooperation in continuing the good work. Whatever of value there may have been in that address to my old comrades at our recent reunion in Columbia (which you seem to endorse by this reception) is due to its pervading idea of Forgetfulness of the Past, Reconciliation in the Present, and Hope for the Future."

General Logan spoke only a few more words. There were other comrades in arms on the speakers' list and he wanted to hear what they had to say.

When the meeting was over he slipped away as quietly as possible, rejoining his father who was awaiting him. Judge Logan had returned to Charleston after staying most of the time with Mully in Richmond from 1871 to 1874. He was now growing feeble at seventy-one years of age and had been obliged to abandon his work as Judge of the City Court of

Charleston. Writing about his stay in her home, Kate had thus described her father-in-law:[xlviii]

"His presence in this household was a benediction; he was a gentleman of the old school, with all of its virtues and none of its faults. His appearance was very attractive, his manner dignified but most cordial and unaffected. It would be difficult to describe a personality more rare and more apart from this day and time. His intense refinement and thoughtfulness for the comfort of others were marked traits, as I can testify. To the servants he was kind and gentle, for with all his learning he had a mind and heart capable of taking in the entire human family as part and parcel of his life. His own people were to him sources of great delight and upon them he lavished his heart's riches."

Mully felt his father's arm leaning on his own affectionately but heavily and realized how weak the Judge had become. Mully had looked forward to this reunion which he had imagined would be so happy, but which now filled him with wistful sadness. All of Charleston gave him this same feeling of nostalgia. Now, walking down Meeting Street, memories of his pre-war days crowded thick upon him. His heart beat fast when he passed the site of the South Carolina Institute Hall in which the Ordinance of Secession had been signed, December 20, 1860.

During the early seventies, General Grant, formerly head of the Armies that had scrapped the idea of secession, was President of the United States. He was in his second term of office and there was much talk of his trying again for election. The third term was most antagonistic to Southerners, because Grant to them had always been associated with War and the "bloody shirt."[6]

General Logan, among many others, had taken up his pen to denounce this third term idea. In two editorials, in the Manchester, Va. Courier for August 22nd and September 26th, 1874, he had upheld his opinions in the following words:

"We feel little apprehension that the third term movement will be successful, but we desire to record our solemn protest against the attempt to ignore one of the most sacred usages of government." In concluding the August editorial, he wrote: "We submit that the present incumbent is ineligible for re-election to the Presidency for a third term, and we trust that an enlightened public opinion will condemn any attempt to secure his nomination. Should he, however, receive the nomination from either or any party we will expect to see the illegal innovation defeated overwhelmingly at the polls."

This editorial is especially interesting today because the third term possibilities of then and now belong to opposing political parties.

---

[6] A term used after the War by politicians and others with political grievances to remind voters of those lost during the War. The term was used by both North and South.-Ed.

Chapter IX

Finding a Keynote—Nationalization 1875-1877

Mully was delighted to be back with his family. How odd it was that not Charleston, but Richmond, now seemed to him to be home.

The morning after his return he awakened in time to walk to his office on Main Street. It had rained the night before and it was now early enough to be cool, even in July. He started over the bridge and walked half way across the river as far as wooded Mayo's Island, whence he could see the view on either bank of the James. On the north side was Richmond with its seven hills-like Rome. Below, the harbor was crowded with schooners. Dense black smoke from steamboats and riverside factories blended in an atmosphere of commercial progress and prosperity. A loud whistle made Mully turn around. He had his usual thrill at sight of an engine proudly drawing its train across the nearby bridge of the Richmond and Petersburg railroad. He remembered hearing that the original structure built in 1838 had been nicknamed the "Noblest bridge in America."[xlix] He remembered his own shock at seeing its ruins soon after the "Fall of Richmond," and his pleasure in watching its rebuilding. How delighted all the townspeople had been to see the bridge in use again just a year after the surrender!

The thought of that year of 1866 made him turn his gaze southward toward his former Manchester home, still standing proudly on a bluff above the river. He loved to think of those early days! But how young he had been then and how groping.

As he turned his glance again toward the North side of the James, he could see the steeples of churches of all denominations, for Richmond was always a city of churches. Sharper than the others his own St. Paul's spire seemed to cut into the sky.

Near the steeple of St. Paul's, he could barely see a corner of his own house on Seventh Street. This brought him back to his life of today, ten years after the war. Wasn't he still groping? What was he accomplishing? For instance, take his South Carolina speeches! His friends had praised him but had he reached any real conclusions? What was the point he needed to make clear in future talks? Did we all spend our lives groping? His own Kate seemed to know what she wanted-to work for her children, her husband, her home, her garden. Even little Katy always knew what she wanted-just to be on the go. If he could only be satisfied with things like that! But mustn't we all grope before we accomplish anything? "What is the matter with me?" Mully wondered. Even Kate's eager admiration could not comfort him.

Kate still loved to read reviews of Mully's work. She always distrusted criticism but believed implicitly every word written in favor of her General.

"See what I have!" she said to Mully one evening in the library. She was wearing a Watteau tea gown of soft grey mull. It was trimmed with lace and had puffed sleeves and a box-plaited ruffle at the bottom. Kate who was interested in history called it her Eighteenth Century costume. She now stood behind Mully and covered his eyes with her hands.

"How can I see with my two eyes bandaged? Am I like Argus with a hundred orbs?"

"I just wanted you to hear what the Enquirer says about you. It's quoted from a South Carolina newspaper."[l] Before he could reply she began:

"'General T.M. Logan bears no resemblance to his namesake, General John A. Logan of Illinois. The orator of the Hampton Legion is a tall slender gentleman with a soft sweet voice and an easy, natural gesticulation.'" Here Kate gesticulated in anything but an "easy, natural" way-very violently, in fact. Provoked, Mully took the sheet away from her.

She thereupon picked up another paper[li] and went on reading, this time in all seriousness:

"'General Hampton then introduced the orator of the occasion, General T. M. Logan, of whom General Longstreet once said: "He is the best skirmish officer in the Army of Northern Virginia."

"'In personal appearance General Logan is slight and delicately built, with a soft, sweet voice, but which on the battlefield could be heard ringing like a clarion. His speech, "The Future of the South," commenced with a calm, philosophical reasoning upon the political structure and growth of our country, its future prosperity, and the permanency of our republican institutions: the material resources of the North; the individuality of the southern people, their duties, hopes and prospects. He then paid a well-deserved tribute to Wade Hampton. Stonewall Jackson he immortalized as the greatest of the great.

"'For an hour and a half General Logan kept his audience spellbound, and that in a crowded hall, in midsummer, ablaze with light and with the thermometer up above the nineties. He was frequently greeted with loud applause.

"'General Logan showed in his oration, clear reasoning, good judgment, sound logic, elegance of diction, profound thought, and a thorough appreciation of his subject; and it is earnestly commended to the thinking men of the country as conveying and containing the true sentiments of the intelligent younger men who composed the Confederate armies. We envy Virginia the possession of him, but are proud to claim him as a native South Carolinian.'

"Well, they give Virginia some credit anyway!" triumphed Kate. "That's pretty generous of South Carolina! Do you remember, years ago, when I asked you if you would adopt Virginia and ham in place of South Carolina and bacon?" She sat on the stool at his feet and looked up into his face, while her eyes brimmed with mischief.

"Well—"

"You did-didn't you?"

"You naughty girl! You knew all the time I wanted to marry you! And you pretended to be so demure!"

Later, Kate brought him her own copy of Harper's Weekly for August 14, 1875. Then she seated herself in a chair at other side of the table and proudly read:

"'General Logan has the good sense to recognize that an industrial system cannot be overthrown, and a new political and civil order established without confusion and mishap, and he has the sagacity to apprehend that the end of slavery, although produced by so tremendous a convulsion, is the beginning of the real prosperity of his State.'

"Well, I reckon some people in the North as well as the South think well of my clever General."

"I wouldn't have much trouble getting ahead if my audiences were composed of Kate Cox Logans! By the way, where is your last Harper's Magazine?"

This remark was meant to tease Kate, for each month she had been looking forward with eagerness to the appearance in Harper's Magazine of a new installment of George Eliot's Daniel Deronda. The March 1876 number would carry the Eleventh Chapter of Book Two of this serial. But little did Daniel Deronda really mean to Kate now, for the same number would also bring something more exciting.

When the magazine did at last arrive late in February, Kate almost tore the pages in her anxiety to find what she was looking for. There was George Eliot again on Page 594, but that was not what she wanted. Turning to the sheet just before that she saw at last the signature, T.M. Logan, and at the top of the page the title: "The Southern Industrial Prospect." With trembling fingers she found the beginning on Page

589 and read with as much eagerness as if she had not worked over the whole piece with Mully months before.

On February 25th she found a review of the article in the Evening Journal:

"Harper's Magazine for March, for which we are indebted to Messrs. West Johnson & Company, contains an ably written article by General T.M. Logan of this city, on the Industrial Prospects in the Southern States. The writer, who has evidently studied political economy to some purpose as well as the Industrial condition of the Southern States, takes a decidedly hopeful view of the future of Southern Industry and gives good reason for the faith that is in him."

"Not enough praise," Kate complained to herself.

But the article bore fruit, as shown by this letter from the middle west:

Office of Indianapolis Journal of Commerce

Indianapolis
May 13, 1876

General T.M. Logan
Richmond, Virginia
Dear Sir:

I have read your remarks upon the industrial condition of the South several times over-and I am very much impressed therewith. I am contemplating taking up my residence in some one of the near Southern States in an effort to awaken the country to the importance of making it practical for the people to engage in all the diversified pursuits which make a nation great and prosperous. The duty on sugar should be so high as to enable the Southern trio of states to enter its production successfully-so with every article of food or clothing or mechanics necessary to the nation so far as possible. I think the great cause of our disaster now is that we have paid all our earning to foreign nations for so many years in exchange for what we should have provided for ourselves. This is the evil to be remedied. Pardon the liberty I take in addressing you, but I believe this to be the policy which is to bring prosperity to the nation and would like to encourage it. I believe a national party ignoring the false political issues of the present time, letting bygones be bygones, and uniting for the development of our National resources would have a wonderful success.

Truly, S.S. Boyee.

"There it is! There it is!" cried Logan excitedly. "That's my future Keynote!"

For once, Kate was slower than Mully. Hopelessly she gazed around the dear, familiar library as if looking for something she had lost. "What is it, dear?" she asked with unusual humility.

"'Can't you guess? What we need today more than all else is Nationalization!'"[7]

"My, what a big word! Do you mean the South is to merge with the North in—in everything? Are we to forget the War and all the South has suffered?" Kate's eyes were wide with shocked surprise. "And you a South Carolinian!"

"Even South Carolinians can be tolerant." His voice was gentler than ever, but it held a hint of reproach.

"Oh, darling, I didn't mean to hurt you. You just took away my breath for the moment. But when I come to think of it, my own father didn't want the Union broken up. Did he tell you how he felt during those dreadful days of suspense in the Spring of 1861?"

"Yes, dear. By the way, how did you find your father when you went to Clover Hill?"

"Oh, I'm terribly worried about him." Kate shook her head sadly. "He's never been the same since Mother left us." Then with one of her sudden changes. "But please tell me what you mean by that overgrown word—Nationalization."

"I mean enmities must not be given the chance to crystallize. As soon and as far as possible we should forget old bitterness. All sections, North, South, East and West, should unite as one. Why should we remain a house divided? I overheard you reading to Muldrup yesterday the tale of the old man and the bundle of sticks. Maybe you read, as we grown-ups often do, without thinking about the context. Anyway, the father scolded his sons for quarrelling. He took a bundle of

---

[7] Unlike the modern connotation, Logan is referring to an appeal for national unity instead of sectionalism.-Ed.

sticks and asked them to break it. They could not. Then he asked them to break each stick separately. This they easily did. 'So with you,' he said. 'Alone you are vulnerable to your weakest enemy. But if you stand together, you are invincible!' Don't you see, my darling, that our own young Nation must stand undivided in the presence of the World of old Nations wiser and more experienced than ourselves?"

Mully was so full of this idea that he soon had his subject prepared. He was fully ready when he went to speak at the Reunion of Hood's Brigade at Waco, Texas, June 27th, 1877.

Kate could not go with him as she was in deep mourning for her father who had died in February. This was a great loss to both her and Mully, for Judge Cox had held an important place in their lives. But they were happy to feel they had had his help and companionship all these past years.

Kate felt a special sadness that her father would not be there to greet the baby soon to arrive. Again a new life was coming to take the place of the one just departed.

Mully arrived in Waco, Texas, early in the morning. The visitors—mostly members of Hood's old Brigade, and the Lone Star Rifles—marched from the train to the McClelland Hotel for breakfast. It was a musical procession, for they were accompanied by the Cadet Cornet Band of Galveston. Logan walked with Major Robert Burns, the secretary of Hood's Brigade Association. Everything wore a holiday air, for the streets were alive with people and flags floated in the breeze. Two hours passed by busily and pleasantly renewing old acquaintances and forming new ones.[lii]

It was not until ten o'clock that the procession was again ready to form. It was soon under way and marched down Austin Street across the square to the junction of Second, where the survivors of Hood's Brigade fell into line, filing into Bridge Street, across the suspension bridge and up to the grounds on the East bank of the Brazos River where the meeting was to take place. Seats for several thousand people, arranged under the shade of live oak trees, formed an amphitheater around a broad platform, soon occupied by the orators of the day, distinguished guests and Press representatives. At eleven o'clock an audience numbering several thousand assembled on the grounds. Then General Logan was introduced as orator of the day. Somehow, this time he did not feel perturbed, so anxious was he to present his views on that subject for which he had so longed searched, Nationalization.

He began his remarks with an allusion to the state he was visiting, and the occasion which called the people together, as well as a touching tribute to General Hood and his comrades in arms. Then he went on:

"No nation has ever been permanently established without some bonds of union to hold its parts together. There must be social cohesion, whether resulting from past associations and the attachments of a common ancestry, or future hopes and the sympathies of a common destiny.

"The first condition of national unity is a nationalized people; but the American people are not nationalized. At the institution of the government, all the conditions seemed favorable to nationality. But differences of interests soon drew sectional lines.

"Naturally, in the development of a nation there are general and common interests tending to union, with local and variant interests tending to disunion; but healthy growth requires that the national life, and the local life, shall both develop freely—neither at the expense of the other.

"Federal authority in America has gradually increased; but this tendency need not destroy constitutional government. Practically, the Hamiltonian system has prevailed; but in fact, the Jeffersonian principles still constitute the law. But to the extremists, North and South, there exists an irreconcilable political antagonism between the so-called Puritan civilization of the North and the Cavalier civilization of the South, which will perpetuate sectional strife. The two principles involved in this American conflict, between Federal and State authority, are identical with those of the Cavalier and the Puritan, respectively, in England. But, strangely enough, the modern Puritan of Massachusetts has ever been on the side of cavalier principles, sustaining the prerogatives of government; while the modern Cavalier of Virginia has been on the side of Puritan principles restraining the prerogatives of government. What folly then, to talk of antagonism in this country between Puritan and Cavalier politics! The struggle between Federal and State authority will continue; but it need not divide a country along geographical lines.

"There is, in short, no political antagonism between North and South which need necessarily continue sectionalism in politics, or prevent the nationalization of America.

"The work of peace and reconciliation is progressing; but Bourbons[8], North and South, still agitate old issues. The American people do not propose that extremists shall dominate this country; but their struggle for dominion has not ceased. Partisan Republicans still appeal to old prejudices, hoping to perpetuate distrust, and arouse the apprehensions of the North. At the same time the Bourbons of the South continue true to their old instincts; and if their counsels unhappily prevailed, harmony could never be restored. Time is doing its healing work; but Bourbonism, North and South, must be suppressed before reconciliation can be complete.

"Suppress all sectionalism; and we become a united nation. We speak the same mother-tongue; and we have drawn our principles of philosophy and law, of liberty and learning from the same headwaters of truth.

"Let common hopes and aspirations, worthy of the American people, animate our purposes. Let statesmanship and patriotism, North, South, East and West, harmonize all differences; and by establishing American Nationality, perpetuate American freedom."

On this Texas speech, only part of which has been quoted, the Richmond Dispatch of July 3rd, 1877, made the following comment:

"General T.M. Logan, of this city, better deserves the title of statesman than most of the gentlemen

---

[8] Colloquially, this referred to the wealthy, conservative, self-styled American aristocracy.-Ed.

who, being in Congress or in high office, are so denominated. His address before the Association of Hood's Texas Brigade at Waco, Texas, June 27th, is a production the like of which few men could write. It is entirely unlike the conventional military oration. It is full of evidences of profound thought. We have but a slight acquaintance with the young orator, but we think that we can safely say that his fine talents ought to be utilized by the people of Richmond."

The Petersburg Appeal (Virginia) had this to say:

"General Logan is not only one of the profoundest and most accurate thinkers in this State, but is a gentleman of untiring energy, extensive attainments, and great modesty. He was one of the youngest and most gallant officers in the Confederate service, and fought himself to the rank of Brigadier-General at the early age of twenty-four. We are glad that the people of Richmond are beginning to recognize his worth, and they would do well to utilize it in their service."

There were so many comments on this speech coming from both North and South that Kate could hardly keep up with them. But she was delighted with the letters which she pounced upon as her own. She always loved to write and receive letters.

Chapter X

Education and Progress
1876-1877

General Logan felt that Nationalization depended most of all on education. Kate begged him to accept an offer to speak before the Educational Association of Virginia, on July 6th, 1876. But Mully was so stricken by the death of his little namesake—less than two months before—that he declared he could not get his mind even on a favorite subject. Kate put aside her own sorrow in trying to turn her husband's thoughts away from his grief. She gained his reluctant consent to work up the paper so that he could appear before the Association later.

The lecture was entitled, "Education and Progress." An excerpt:

"The springs of social progress all have their success in the lower strata of society. The upper ranks of human life are naturally conservative; the lower ranks are instinctively progressive. The apparent interests and traditions of the one are opposed to all reforms, while the aims and aspirations of the other all lead to change. The spirit of reform, thus dwelling with the masses of the people, as their power to reform increases, the knowledge to reform wisely must also be increased; and hence again with the gradual transition of power from the higher to the lower strata, it becomes more and more important to educate all classes of the people."

In another part of the speech General Logan was even more forward-looking, giving a hint of the Social Credit idea of today:

"Many of the objections which have been urged against popular education apply only to the transition state through which it is still passing, for the full fruits are not to be expected in one generation, or several generations, but are to be reaped ultimately in the improvement of the race.

"As a matter of justice, the laborer is entitled to some benefit from the increased control of man over nature, resulting from the advance of human knowledge; and accordingly with the greater facilities for accumulating the necessaries of life, the industrial classes could reasonably claim, as their portion of the fruits, more time and opportunity for self-improvement."

One summer afternoon Mully was working on a speech at home in the library, as he often loved to do. Kate entered. She said, "You haven't written a word yet about the education of women!"

After some bantering, he admitted he had. He began reading to her: "In the lower grades of instruction, the two sexes under our civilization probably enjoy equal advantages; but in the higher grades, the approved methods of female education usually exclude the higher forms of knowledge, and do not contemplate the highest mental training. While under this so-called education of woman no efforts are spared to make her 'accomplished,' little attention is paid to developing the reasoning faculties; and in consequence, she is proverbially guided by impulse and not by reason.

"It is urged, however, that the highest education of the intellect is opposed in woman to the purest qualities of the heart; and that it is more desirable to develop her emotional nature than to cultivate her mental powers. But, it is not true that strength of mind in woman is incompatible with simplicity of character. On the contrary, the development of her mental faculties will elevate her womanly qualities, on the same principle that increased intelligence produces higher and purer phases of morals and of religion.

"It is a significant fact in this connection, that in the course of human progress all great advances have been accompanied, if not always caused, by social changes which elevated the position of woman. And it would not be venturing far to predict a new era of advance, whenever public sentiment outgrowing traditionary prejudices as to the education of woman and her sphere, shall require her intellectual powers to be cultivated and developed by suitable education. Also, by modifying the habits and usages of society, afford her greater opportunities for using her talents in suitable avocations."

Mully paused a moment, and then continued:

"After this thought of education and progress, suggesting vast bounds as the limits of human progress during the allotted life-time of humanity, I might venture, if the occasion were appropriate, beyond the sphere of pure reason: and, invoking the aid of the imagination with its conceptions of untold possibilities for man in the coming centuries, I might seek to picture in the mind, as not unreasonable expectation, an epoch of social harmony and perfection in the distant eons of the future, corresponding to that period of peace and happiness on earth which the ancient prophets have predicted."

It is interesting to note that Mully, in speaking hopefully, used the expression "distant eons of the future." Though an idealist he was far too practical to believe that the perfect state could be attained by tearing up all the old maxims overnight and starting out the next morning with a brand new shiny book of untested proverbs.

He concluded thus:

"So far, in defining the influence which education may exert on human progress, I have contemplated only particular civilizations; but as the effect of education is also cumulative from generation to generation, so also it is cumulative from civilization to civilization. As habits and aptitudes of the individual are transmitted from generation to generation, so also are the habits and aptitudes of the race.

"Therefore in the decline and fall of one civilization, all seems lost, yet whatever is valuable is preserved for the coming race. Only those characteristics take root and live which are congenial to the young and uncorrupted nation. All degenerative qualities perish with the civilization; while those which are invigorating survive, and, received as seeds in the soil of a new social era, they germinate and grow in greater strength, and as inheritances from the old civilization contribute to the progress of the new.

"Progressive countries are forced to adopt some system of public instruction, or be distanced in the industrial race of the nations."

This speech received favorable comment in the New York World, September 7th, 1877, and in the Springfield, Mass., Daily Republican of same date. This was evidence that the work of Southern progressive leaders was penetrating into the strongholds of the North.

"Education and Progress" also called forth a letter from the American Social Science Association of Boston, Mass. It was signed by S.B. Sanborn, Secretary, and invited Mully to read a paper before the Association at Saratoga, September 6th, 1877. The general subject under discussion was the question of education in the Southern States. Mully accepted and decided to call his paper, "The Opposition in The South To The Free School System."

In order to obtain the proper viewpoint he corresponded with S.C. Armstrong, Principal of the (Colored) Hampton Normal and Agricultural Institute at Hampton, Virginia. Here are some of Mr. Armstrong's ideas:

"To coddle the negro is as bad as to kick him. He has had too much of both.

"He (the negro) is impatient of taking each round of the ladder up—but wishes to jump to the top at once. The colored student would generally be glad to omit spelling and begin with Greek. But he has some fine, strong, interesting points."

Both Kate and Mully felt very sad while working up this paper. The subject has been a favorite one with Judge Cox and they knew how he would have loved to help. Kate read over and over again the parts of the lecture which she thought would appeal most to her father.

"The negro formerly exerted a beneficial influence on society, although limited race education and advantages accounted more than all else for the fact that he occupied a lower plane. Therefore the influence of the freedmen now as a distinct class of laborers should tend more strongly to elevate the white race."

And later, "For more than a century the vexed question of the negro has perplexed the first intellects of the South. But the freedman is now a citizen and voter; and self-interest should prompt the whites to prepare him for greater usefulness.

"As a laborer ignorance is his greatest deficiency; this would soonest be removed by the free school system.

"As a voter, the freedman is liable, from ignorance, to be misled by demagogues; but when taught to read he is brought within the influence of the Press. Therefore his greatest deficiency as a voter would be removed by the free school system.

"All of the arguments usually advanced in favor of public instruction apply with greater force in the case of the negro. And thus every consideration of the subject leads to the conclusion that the future welfare and prosperity of the South demand the education of the freedman by public school instruction."

Kate was delighted with the reviews of this lecture. She expected the Northern ones to be favorable, but was a little doubtful as to what they would say in the South, especially in General Logan's native state. She therefore read with great pride a notice in the Charleston News and Courier for September 14th, 1877:

"As a native Southerner who won distinction in the most brilliant campaigns of the War, General Logan is entitled to a respectful hearing by his own people and as an earnest and thoughtful student, who has devoted much time and labor to the subject of which he speaks, and as a public man whose liberal and enlarged views on other subjects are already well known, he must command the attention of the whole country."

On November 6th, 1877, there arrived at the Logan home a very tiny baby. She weighed only about three pounds and the clothes prepared for her overwhelmed her completely. Resourceful sister Katy bustled into her own room, returning shortly with a complete doll's outfit for the new arrival. But clothes do not always make the man—nor the baby either. If Kate had been one whit less vigorous, a fraction less devoted, the miniature baby could not have survived!

Mully's artistic sister, Lily, who was staying at the Logan's at the time and shared a great tenderness for the baby, threw out hints for giving the little one her own name—or names. Kate, however, favored neither Josephine Maria nor Lily for the baby, so she thought out a pleasant alternative.

"I'll ask Lily to be godmother and give her a choice of names. She certainly wouldn't choose her own!"

But Kate reckoned without her sister-in-law, who eagerly accepted the place of godmother, but insisted at the same time that the baby be called Lily, and as little Katy said, the name "stack." Only she was called Lilybud to distinguish her from her godmother.

With each of their children's individualities strongly defined, the parents felt a very personal interest in the subject of education. "If members of one family are so different," Mully asked Kate, "how can educators expect to succeed with children of varied families and nationalities, by throwing them all into one stereotyped mould?

It was this feeling of the sacredness of personality which made the General try to interfere as little as possible with the development of the separate individualities of his own children.

Chapter XI

Partly Political
1878-1880

On a June afternoon in 1878, Mully saw for the first time an invention of Mr. Thomas Edison's. Mully loved all new "contraptions" so he was especially interested in this phonograph by which sounds could be reproduced, not just once at the same time as in the instrument called a telephone. Instead, this phonograph made the sounds into a permanent record. The idea fascinated Mully beyond words and he pondered the possibilities of this new machine. He could hardly wait to get home and put down his impressions in his brown notebook. That night as soon as supper was over he went to his study and began to write:

"There is nothing new under the sun. In this age of new inventions, of telegraphs and steam transportation, of telephones and phonographs, we are apt to disbelieve the wise man's adage, although this illustrates a profound truth of human life. If history does not in fact repeat itself, we find that in the ever changing course of human events like influences and circumstances produce like events, and in the downfall of nations and civilizations, old conditions are constantly recurring."

Here he paused, not knowing how to proceed. We can hardly believe that this was written in 1878, so close a parallel to present day thought does it present.

Kate now entered the study. She was wearing a blue silk all-in-one dress. It had close-fitting lines from high ruffed neck to about the knee. Here were bunched a group of Roman striped folds. Below these folds a box-pleated ruffle swept the ground. The long tight sleeves ending ruching, matching the neck ruff. Her soft wavy hair was drawn back in a chignon, graced by a tall black comb, trimmed in blue enamel to match her dress.

"How do you like my Princess gown?" Kate asked, sweeping around in a rather hampered circle, to the accompaniment of swishing skirts. She had an evening journal in hand. "And what's all this I see in the paper about Communism?"

Mully looked up from his writing tablet. He had expected to resent an interruption but now he was delighted. "My dear child, what a wonder you are! You're always suggesting ideas for me to write about. If you can keep your lively little tongue quiet, I'll explain."

"Explain about what?"

"But, darling, have you forgotten your own question? About Communism, of course."

"No wonder I forgot. That's a brand new subject—isn't it? Like my dress for instance?"

"There's nothing new under the sun," Mully repeated cryptically. "But your two subjects are as different as night from day. Your dress denotes a finished—almost an effete civilization. Communism[liii] on the contrary, is only an attempt to reorganize society on its most primitive basis. Common ownership was the first form under which property was held, when clothing was at its simplest. Communism, you see, is really far older than separate ownership."

"I never would have thought that," said Kate.

Mully went on. "If we should try to reorganize society on the basis of communism, we should have to lose the mellowing influences of civilized society, returning to the primitive conditions of our barbarian ancestors. This would mean going back even further than the village communities of India or the communal townships of old Russia. Not only would individual property be destroyed but also that of the family and tribe.

"No one would strive without either compulsion or payment. If work didn't put people forward most of them wouldn't make any effort. Selfish human nature as it now exists would perish without the principle of separate ownership of property."

"But why shouldn't human nature improve and become unselfish?" asked Kate. "Then every man would work for others and altruism could take the place of competition in the future?"

"Oh, as for the future, my dear, yes, all that may come in some far distant time. But we human beings have a great deal of inertia and so we have to be pushed into work. Competition and the longing for private ownership are our goads today. You see, we are all naturally lazy."

"You lazy! I never heard such a thing!" Kate was indignant. "I'm lazy, you mean." She jumped up briskly. "I hear the baby crying." She began to run up the steps as swiftly as her tight skirt would allow. Mully followed her. He loved to visit his children in the nursery.

Later[liv] he took up the history of Communism as he had read about it in the recent papers and wrote again in his notebook:

"A few weeks after the July, 1877 riot, the socialistic or workingmen's party held a convention in Cincinnati and laid down an extremely communistic platform. But the old party organizations still continued to poll a vast majority of votes. During the summer the German socialistic Congress by a large majority voted extreme communistic doctrines. In January of this year the French Workingmen's Congress met at Lyons and surprised the world by the moderate views they expressed. In many instances this last meeting was a remarkable one. It indicates that the extreme doctrines of communism which had their birth in France are not as strong with the workmen as they were. The workmen themselves at this meeting openly repudiated such communistic doctrines and such leaders as Louis Blanc, Proudhon, Victor Hugo and others. Experience has made them more practical. An able resume of the proceedings of this Congress will be found in the May number of the Fortnightly Review by Frederick Harrison. In the January number of the British Quarterly review will be found extracts from the platform of the Cincinnati and the German meetings in an article on Capital and Labor.

"The attempted assassination of the Emperor William has again given prominence to the socialistic doctrines, and it is apparent that extreme views are still held in Germany, and this influence is extending.

"The recent election in San Francisco awakened a great interest in communism in America. The Herald has already sounded the alarm in a series of sensational leaders.

"Communism is certainly one of the leading social and political questions of our day.

"There is no doubt that there exist today many cruel defects for which socialistic remedies are urged. Friends of order and authority should seek the causes and attempt to remove them, or at least provide some palliation.

"Otherwise they must be warned that it is an axiom of social science that an unequal distribution of wealth will be followed by an unequal distribution of social and political power, and that the effect will be stagnation, decline, and ultimately decay and ruin."[lv]

It seems strange that General Logan with such far-seeing ideas should have been invited in 1879 to be Chairman of the Virginia Conservative Party. This same post had been offered in 1870 to Judge Cox. He had refused because of ill health.

Kate wanted to know if the General would accept this Chairmanship.

"Of course I shall," he declared. "You must remember that I have been championing this cause since 1874. I said in an editorial then[lvi] and I still repeat: If the conditions of Virginia today are better than that of other Southern States it is due to the Conservatives. As you may remember this party was started to oppose the radical rule which threatened this State with ruin."

"But what about our Richmond City Council of 1870? Didn't they force out those hateful military appointees and put our own people in their places? Isn't that what cut short the hours of reconstruction here?"

"Yes, that Council was a wonderful help, of course, but only for the city. The Conservative Party was also for the State. My dear child, don't you realize that the 'bloody shirt' anti-South Republicans still have a strangle-hold on the party? They will have to be defeated by some combination embracing every element of opposition and disaffection rather than by the Democratic party alone, under its present name and organization. The time has now arrived for Virginia and the South to cooperate actively with the opposition. Such a movement to be successful must originate with the Democratic leaders."

While Mully was discussing the methods of breaking the absolute reign of hide-bound republicanism, the "Union Forever Rule of the Bloody-Shirt" issue was about to tear the party apart from its own inner dissension. The Republicans in the North still had everything their own way in those days and nomination was almost the same election. But there came the rub! Nomination was no longer a simple matter. The eight years under Grant and the "Union Forever" militarists had been the richest ever for political patronage. But those milder Republicans who had been left off the pork-barrel list, were eager to nose in and have their share.

Thus the Republican convention of 1880 was full of bitter recriminations between the Grant and the anti-Grant forces. As we all know the latter non-Militarists were finally successful. Senator elect, James A. Garfield, after a masterly speech, became the Man of the Hour. He was nominated and later elected but not by an overwhelming vote. Of course, no one knew then how soon his triumph would be cut short by death. In any case, the Bloody-Shirts were out, and the whole country had a much better chance of becoming amalgamated into one nation.

General Logan's intense desire to see the amalgamation into one nation of his so recently divided country was what awakened his mind to the subversive influences of Communism as show earlier in this chapter. "Common ownership," he said, "would destroy ambition, as no one would strive without either compulsion or payment."

But Communism seemed to him no greater threat to American ideas than what he called "the apprehended danger of Caesarism." Under a government of Dictators he saw again the individual's loss of ambition and initiative. "Self-government," he wrote, "is the centralizing idea of America's being. To vindicate the sovereignty of her people is her first responsibility."

What a lesson this is to us to-day (sic); threatened as we are by idealogies (sic) and totalitarian governments.

Chapter XII

Humpty-Dumpty or No?
1877-1883

General Logan's interest in education and politics continued, but the problems of transportation also occupied much of his time and thought. He liked to look down from the bridge at the tow-path of the canal of the James River and Kanawha Coal Company. He knew that this waterway had been chartered in 1832, with John Marshall as Chairman, though the original project for a canal, under the name of "James River Company" had been incorporated in 1784.

In 1835 a plan was adopted to enlarge the canal between Richmond and Maiden's Adventure and to continue it to Lynchburg, so that one could proceed to the Kanawha River and thence to Ohio. By 1841, the capacity of the canal was increased to float boats of sixty tons.

In 1877, the canal was damaged by a freshet. Thereafter General Logan and many other Richmonders thought it would be best abandon it, substituting a railroad for 231 miles along the towpath as far as Clifton Forge, Virginia. Three years later (1880) this was accomplished, when the Richmond and Allegheny Rail Road bought the canal with all of its property. Later, this was taken over by the Chesapeake and Ohio.

General Logan guessed nothing of that later development on a May morning in 1877 when he stood at the packet boat landing at the foot of Eighth Street. He enjoyed the busy scene of embarcation, with passengers arriving and baggage being stored away. He saw the packet pushed under the bridge at Seventh Street. There he watched the horses being hitched. He was startled for the hundredth time at the terrific jerk with which it began its way up stream. He continued to watch the packet until it had rounded Penitentiary Hill to disappear from view. What worried Mully was the thought that it would be ten days before the cheering crowd reached Lynchburg, only about one hundred and fifty miles away. This lack of speed was even more of a problem with the freight bateaux, which travelled much more slowly, as most of them were poled by hand.

The General had come to the river this morning to obtain the proper viewpoint before his proposed speech of welcome to a group of about one hundred and twenty-five businessmen from the Middle West. They had gathered first at Cincinnati for the trip to Richmond, Norfolk, and points further South.[lvii]

They took the packet boat from Cincinnati to Huntington and there boarded a Chesapeake and Ohio Railroad train. They were met at Kanawha Falls by a small group from Richmond and were joined by a larger group of Richmond men when they stopped over at the famous White Sulphur Springs.

By eight o'clock on the night of May 11th, a large crowd had assembled at the Chesapeake and Ohio depot to meet the men of the West.[lviii] They arrived about half past eight amid shouts of welcome. The excursionists moved on to the platform of the cars and Mr. Pulliam, President of the Home Delegation, introduced them to Mayor Carrington, who, standing on a step of the ticket office, extended to them a sincere invitation to share in the hospitality of Richmond.

Next in turn Captain C. M. Holloway of Cincinnati, spoke from the platform. He expressed his appreciation of the cordial reception given his party by the Richmond representatives. He and his group then descended from the train and, together with the home delegation, formed a procession headed by Kessnich's band. Accompanied by stirring music they all marched to the Exchange Hotel. During that evening they amused themselves informally. Some went to the hop at Ford's Hotel, some strolled about the City, while the more easily fatigued went to bed.

The following day, about ten o'clock, they began to assemble in the gentlemen's parlor of the Exchange Hotel. There was no speechmaking but everybody was chatting and handshaking in a most friendly manner. Certainly all war feeling had disappeared by now!

Captain L.L. Bass, Marshal of the day, called the assemblage to order about half past ten and soon the whole procession, Westerners and Richmonders together, locked arms and moved in double file to the Capitol. A quarter of an hour later they entered the

House of Delegates. The galleries were soon packed by citizens, including many women, and Kessnich's band enlivened the scene and stirred the enthusiasm of the gathering.

The house was called to order and the representatives of the Press were asked to act as secretaries. The Mayor made a few welcoming remarks. The chosen orator of the day, General T.M. Logan, was next introduced. It may be seen by this choice that the General's name had now become thoroughly identified with the railroad developments in Richmond. That was why he had been selected as speaker at this reception to the "Men of the West" who had come to Richmond to further a prospect for development of "trade avenues between the Western Valley and the Atlantic Seaboard" along what is now the Chesapeake and Ohio railroad.

Logan's speech welcomed the "Westerners" as allies and friends of the people of the South and stressed the mutual benefits of the two sections could bestow on each other. Then he went on to say: "You come at an auspicious time. This City has looked forward for years to the completion of the Chesapeake and Ohio Railroad as a means of insuring [sic] communication with your cities. Virginia regards you as her offspring. Our people all look to your people as their kinsmen, their natural allies, and their business friends. Virginia and her Western daughters have a common destiny of brilliant promise."

After explaining more fully the definite advantages to be gained by this linking of East and West, General Logan continued with these words: "The Southern States all seek, severally, closer business relations with your people, while the South as a whole, on grounds of public policy, and of common justice asks your aid and cooperation for the construction of a Southern highway to the Pacific as a work of national importance."

The meeting bore fruit, for the cooperation of the two sections of the country became an assured success.

This was really a turning point in Logan's career.

By the next year his railroad interest was becoming definite. He was gradually giving up his other legal work in favor of the Richmond and Danville railroad, which had been originally chartered in 1847. At last his opportunity to work for railway expansion in the South had arrived.

He hurried home early one day, sat down in his study and waited impatiently to discuss the situation with Kate, who had not yet come in. It was a winter afternoon and the fire was burning brightly in the grate. Soon Kate entered briskly, throwing down her short black beaded cape. She was wearing the dull black Watteau style silk of two years before, but the dress was not conspicuous now, for the fashions of the day had grown up to match it. Her new hat, however, was still rather extreme. It was a tight, dark silk bonnet perched on her head in the shape of an inverted bird-nest. Near the front three jet ornaments stuck up in the air like the last leaves topping an autumn tree.

Mully was too interested in his own affairs to remark on the rather outlandish hat. As soon as Kate had taken it off and settled in her chair, he began to consult her. "What do you think about my idea of working toward an increase of the mileage of the Richmond and Danville? This would make Richmond a real railway center."

Kate sprang up and kissed him on the forehead. "You smart General," she said. Then settling back into her chair she went on soberly. "But it makes things difficult for me. First I had to become accustomed to a soldier for a husband. Then I had to adjust my ideas to a lawyer and a speaker. Now it's to be a railway president!"

"Not so fast!" he interposed. "This is only the beginning. Maybe I'll never be a president."

"I know better, General." She was positive.

"One trouble in expanding the line," he told her, "is that the different roads I want to bring into a possible new combine are not all in this state. The law says the Richmond and Danville corporation couldn't hold interstate lines."

But there's a way out?"

"Yes, I've thought about that. I'll change the name of the Company and ask for a new interstate charter."

Mammy came to the door. "The baby wants you, Miss Kate."

Little Lena, born September 2nd, 1879, never had given her parents a second worry. She was bounding with health and overflowing with goodness. Katie, Meta, Jimmy and tiny Lilybud were all her adorers. "Don't you spoil my baby!" Mammy was always counseling. Mammy (Ellen Jasper) had been in the family service since the birth of Katie and her word was law, even with Mrs. Logan. The children adored Mammy with just the right admixture of wholesome fear.

At this time General and Mrs. Logan were living at 14 West Franklin Street. The Hobsons lived at the other end of the block and the Frederic R. Scotts were staying next door, while their new house at 712 West Franklin, opposite Monroe Park, was being built. The 700 block was then considered almost out of town and the Scott's new home was about the largest brick house in Richmond.

The West Franklin Street house was set back in a large yard and had a wide iron railed piazza where the children loved to play ship. On the right, as one entered, were the front and back parlors with a large dining room behind. On the left was the General's study and behind that the sitting room. The children had "high tea" there every afternoon at six—beaten biscuit, chicken and jam. Sometimes remaining for tea was the French governess, Madame Guillame. She was a dear old woman with waxen skin, deep brown eyes, and beautiful hands. She taught Katie to read French at sight.

The young people loved to stand at the window and watch the street traffic of the day whirl by. Most exciting of all was to see Mrs. Phillip Haxall, the famous beauty of the 70's and 80's, drive by daily in her shining Victoria. While she was still the lovely Mary Triplett, the last duel in Virginia is said to have been fought for her favor. The combatants were John Mordecai and Page McCarthy[sic][9].

---

[9] The Mordecai-McCarty duel, fought in the Oakwood Cemetery in 1872, ended with Mordecai dead and his former friend McCarty badly wounded and emotionally devastated.-Ed

Mully did not want to bore Kate with figures, so he waited until the next day at the office to make his calculations about the additions to the Richmond and Danville. He put down on a piece of paper the list of railroads he wanted to combine:

The Virginia Midland---------------------------412 miles
The Georgia Pacific----------------------------317 miles
The Western North Carolina------------------274 miles
The Columbia and Greenville----------------196 miles
The Charlotte, Columbia and Augusta----191 miles

This list with other shorter lines, would in the aggregate make a total of 1,838 miles.

But here came a big hitch. After Logan studied and restudied the R&D Charter, he was obliged to come to this devastating conclusion: the new mileage would take the road beyond the State lines and the Charter was strictly inter-state! Suddenly he had an idea. He called his associates together and they discussed the following plan.

"Why not," asked the General, "apply for a new Charter? We'll mass all our holdings together under a different name."

The plan was accepted with enthusiasm. There was discussion back and forth until finally there evolved a name for the proposed combined holdings:

"The Richmond and West Point Terminal Railway and Warehouse Company." This was henceforth familiarly called the "Terminal Company."

On March 8th, 1880, a charter of broad significance was obtained for this Company by the Counsel, Colonel W.W. Gordon.[lix] The Richmond News Leader gives the picture of Mr. Gordon: "When he applied at Columbia, S.C., for admission to the part of the court room reserved for lawyers, indicated by a railing, the court official would not let him in and he quietly took his seat on the outside. The other lawyers, representing various railroad interests opposed to confirmation, made their addresses and wound up by saying that there seem to be no lawyer representing the purchaser. Colonel Gordon then got up, told them who he was, that he represented the "Terminal" Company, had heard the arguments, and was ready to reply. The Court and the lawyers were profuse in their apologies.

The table was covered with books of the other lawyers, and Colonel Gordon, by reference to them, got a decision confirming the sale. The Greenville and Columbia became thus a part of the system and has ever since so remained."

Meanwhile Logan and another Confederate veteran, Major James H. Dooly[sic], were gradually buying up the Richmond and Danville stock. A great part of the equity was owned by the Pennsylvania Railroad Company. The Logan crowd obtained an option on this pool at about $55 a share, although the price on the local market was about $65. Logan's associates were at this time, besides Major Dooly, John Stewart of Brook Hill, his brother Daniel, and his son-in-law, Joseph Bryan, Colonel William B. Palmer, Moses Milhiser, and his son Augustus. These men combined with others to purchase the pool at the option price.[lx]

In the Charleston, S.C. Sunday News, December 12th, 1886, a picturesque view of the Richmond and Danville deal is given:

"In Richmond, Virginia, where General Logan is as well know as he is at home in South Carolina, nearly everybody had an interest in the Richmond and Danville stock. The women asked for it, the children cried for it. Staid business men were as eager to put their money in the stock as their clerks and salesmen were. The gilded youth of the seven-hilled city cocked their hats and smoked twenty-cent cigars."

The excitement was caused because the formation of the "Terminal Company" had caused the Richmond and Danville stock to rise from under par to as high as two hundred and fifty.

The "Terminal Company" began at once to expand. This combine soon built the Georgia Pacific from Birmingham to the Mississippi River under a charter which allowed it to proceed to the Pacific; bought the Greenville and Columbia (S.C.) Railroad; controlled the roads from Richmond to Birmingham; the Virginia Midland from Washington, D.C. to Danville, Va., and other minor roads in Virginia and North Carolina.

In less than two years the "Terminal Company" increased its trackage to over two thousand.[lxi] The stock went above two hundred and fifty dollars a share.[lxii]

The Charleston New completes the picture: "After having engaged in coal mining and other operations, General Logan interested himself in railroad affairs and became a leader in the combinations which made the movement in Richmond and Danville stock the great excitement of Wall Street. The stock had sold for a mere trifle, but by the combination that were effected by General Logan and his friends, an auxiliary combination—The Richmond and West Point Terminal Company—was formed and the Richmond and Danville stock went whirling up to 250."

Before 1882 General Logan had practically retired from the law. His railroad business kept him in New York most of the time. He wanted to have his family near him, so they spent the summer of 1882 on Long Island at the Babylon Hotel. Oscar Wilde happened to be staying there for a while, and every evening before the music began in the ballroom, he used to amuse the children with stories. Many of these same tales appeared in 1888 under the general title of "The Happy Prince." There were others in the same volume, including "The Birthday of the Infanta" and "The Nightingale and the Rose."

Wilde seemed to know just how to treat young people, and they adored him. They would cluster around him in a corner of the ballroom and even the older boys and girls were disappointed when the music started each evening. They would rather listen to Wilde's sympathetic, varied voice than dance! Why should they object to his funny knee breeches and sweeping light brown hair? And when talking to very young people, he forgot to use his mincing, affected postures.

Children, in relation to aesthetics, became the subject of several of his talks in the hotel dining room. The young people stood so little in awe of the speaker that they scampered around the room during his lecture.

This was all part of his grand tour of America. He had come to New York a few months earlier under the auspices of D'Oyley Carte, representing the Gilbert and Sullivan opera Patience. Bunthorne, the aesthetic poet in the libretto, was everywhere identified with Wilde, who didn't seem to mind the idea of making a monkey of himself as a sort of living (paid) advertisement for the opera.

All winter and spring, he had been running over the country in knickerbockers and braid-edged coats of greenish brown. His costume was further carried out by a high hat and collar from which flowed a rivulet of bright silk for a tie. The effect was completed by pointed shoes with bows and lavender or yellow gloves. When he appeared on the street, he was made even more conspicuous by his great height and a steadily increasing breadth in proportion. At this time he was twenty-eight years old, far from handsome and of a rather pasty complexion. But no one could deny the beauty of his luminous eyes.

He was a humorous, ready speaker. It is a great pity there was no modern recording system in those days, so that those who have never heard him could form some idea of his delightful, sympathetic intonations. He was best of all in ordinary conversations—never at a loss for a quick comeback. He loved to turn sayings upside down and put them the unexpected way, like, "Nothing succeeds like excess." His talks were almost always on aesthetics, which he called the "Science of the Beautiful—a sort of correlation of all the arts."

Parents looked on his oddities indulgently because he was kind to their children. If they laughed at him it was in a spirit of clean fun. One has to remember that this was almost ten years before Wilde's affair with Lord Alfred Douglas (1891 and on).

In 1895, the younger Logans were much shocked to hear of Wilde's imprisonment. They were also mystified by their Mother's purse-lipped refusal to explain why this odd but kindly man should be in jail. There was so little talk in those days about homosexuality that perhaps Mrs. Logan was herself rather confused on the subject. But she did know that whatever it was it was strictly taboo.

The Logans had a lovely time that summer of 1882, boating on the sound, and having clam-bakes and driving around in a hired carriage. Coney Island was then quiet, with no boardwalk or shops, and Mammy used to take the children there to hear Sousa play. It was the first summer he had a band of his own. Mammy loved to dress up all her babies and take them promenading.

In 1883 the family stayed at White Sulphur, and General Logan came down from New York for the weekends. Once he arrived to find the Count of Sibour dancing a waltz with the fifteen-year old Katy. He stood at the ball-room window watching and finally said to Kate: "Mrs. Logan, do you allow your daughter to have a man's arm around her?" The mother reported this remark to her eldest daughter and Katy never danced a step of a round dance again until she was thirty.

Those were gay days at the White Sulphur. Too frivolous, thought Kate, who wanted her children to be unworldly. One night she observed the chattering girls seated in rows watching the dancers. Most of the young people's dresses were white mull or tulle over some color. She saw one child, with a face too sharp for her years, lift the overskirts of her companions to discover if the slips underneath were cotton or silk, and then and there Kate decided that the sooner they moved to the farm they had recently purchased the better for the children, if she wanted to keep them unworldly.

Also, that day at the swimming pool there occurred a rather shocking incident. The pool was in two parts, divided by a fairly opaque barrier, as it was not considered proper for men and women to bathe together. Not even Kate could see the reason why, for the ladies wore suits with long sleeves and full skirts coming up to the knee. On this particular day, lovely Miss A., the belle of White Sulphur, was in fine fettle. A girl companion, who had naughtily visited a New York Variety Show, had remarked in Miss A.'s presence that the belle's er-er-legs were finer than any she'd seen at the New York Show. This gave Miss A. a daring thought. Something happened to her garter while she was in the water.

Just as she left the pool and walked out on land at least four inches of that beautiful leg were visible to the men entering and leaving the water at the end of the barrier. Demurely but slowly she drew on her wrapper and sauntered to her bath house. When she emerged there was a great commotion near the pool. "What has happened?" she wanted to know.

"Your brother has challenged Mr. C. to a duel!"

"Why?" But she had already half guessed.

"Because—well—because Mr. C. said a terrible thing—that you—er—broke your garter on purpose!"

She rushed up to her brother. "That's all right, dear, you needn't fight. I did!"

Another bathing incident occurred a few years later at a Northern resort. Three lovely sisters in bathing suits of the day were reclining on the beach with their swains. This was not quite the thing to do, especially with a society photographer coming to take their pictures. What was their father's horror to see a large copy of the group in a chic magazine of the period? He was a man of property and he felt there could be no better way of spending his money than to cut short this indignity. He bought up the whole issue of the magazine.

The Logans had been happy and prosperous up to this time, but the carefree days would soon be over! Every time Mully came to visit the family he seemed more and more worried. Kate's keen intuition told her something was wrong. For the first time since their marriage he would not confide in her! Hardly had they reached their home in Richmond before the Richmond and Danville Railroad crashed! This was in 1883. And not only the Logans but all of Richmond was to feel the shock. A depressed atmosphere prevailed—different indeed from the earlier days when "the gilded youth of the seven-hilled city cocked their hats and smoked twenty-cent cigars." For almost everyone in Richmond had bought Terminal stock!

"That's what I mind the most," Mully confided sadly to Kate, for he was now not only willing to talk, but he clung to her for help and strength. "I mind it most for those others, the ones who confided in me."

"But you and the railroad will both come back," Kate reminded him.

"Will I? Maybe I'm just a Humpty-Dumpty smashed for good. But if anything can help me it will be you and the children."

"What happened?"

"Jay Gould did it, through the help of his representative, George S. Scott. Our capital was limited, theirs was boundless. They depressed the stock and bought me out."

The General was not one to abuse his neighbors or even his competitors, so he did not say that the squeeze had come through "double-crossing" by some of his supposed friends whom he had originally interested in the company.

The Washington Critic of November 22, 1886 said, "Shortly after the tremendous fall in Richmond and Danville stock, Jay Gould's representative, George S. Scott, bough the controlling interest in both systems, and ousted General Logan and his associates and moved the headquarters to this city. General Logan protested against this, without avail."

The Financial Record of November 20, 1886 had this to say:

"The movement of 1882 in these properties broke down because of the financial disability of its daring projector (General Logan) to carry it to the desired end and not because the properties were held to be valueless. On the contrary, when General Logan withdrew on the failure of the movement, the stock of Danville was bought for a song by the shrewdest and longest-headed people in Wall Street."

Meanwhile the Logan children and servants thought of the crash as a physical cataclysm: "Everything's done busted up," said old Uncle Ben, giving the children an exciting Humpty-Dumpty picture of splintered glass and shells. Led by the adventurous Meta, they went off on a voyage of discovery, ending in mixed disappointment and relief when they found the china closet intact. But they knew something was wrong.

General Logan had never yet seen his farm on the River near Howardsville, about ninety miles above Richmond. Now he decided that the best thing would be to give up the expensive city life and move to the country where they could live more simply. He rented his house to Colonel Rives and went to the Hartsook place near Howardsville. This was afterward bought by Mr. Emil Otto Nolting of Richmond. From their temporary home the Logans could look over the River across the wide stretch of low grounds, up the gentle rise of the hills to the site where their new home, Algoma, was being built.

Compared to former days they were now living very plainly, but from General Logan's behavior the children could never have realized how his dreams had crashed to earth. He followed his own directions to Kate and did not have the least disposition to make his family share his anxieties.

Chapter XIII

The Come Back
1883-1886

I n the crash of 1883 General Logan not only lost all his money, but was temporarily ousted from his position as Vice-President of the Terminal Company.

As "Gath" put it picturesquely in the Cincinnati Enquirer of Nov. 30th, 1886, "The Danville Railroad meant to skin out the Danville Terminal Company and go on and complete its affairs—in its own way." The General's opponent, George S. Scott, even went so far as to say, "Before I get through with Logan he will have to borrow money enough to pay his fare back to Richmond."[lxiii]

But the General was never forced to this sorry pass. Courageously he continued to work and to make all the valuable contacts possible, both in the South and in New York. Among those he interested in New York, was John D. Rockefeller, who refused at that time to take hold, but advised Logan to retire to his farm and keep an eye on the parties who had control and to keep him posted, and at the proper time he would come forward. Logan followed his advice to the letter and for this he was later very thankful.[lxiv]

It was General Logan's philosophy, optimism, and above all, courage that enabled him to come back—for come back he did. He soon proved that share in Richmond and Danville affairs was not a real Humpty-Dumpty, for in three years he put the pieces together in what the newspapers called "Logan's Masterstroke."

If it should be asked why the General, who was so important, was never made President of the Richmond and Danville, the answer will be found in the following quotation from an editorial in The State, Richmond, Va., December 17, 1886.

"Mr. Sully accepted the presidency only after it had been declined by Mr. Pace and General Logan, and accepted it, too, with the assurance that Vice President Logan would be virtually President; so far as the management of the local interests of the line are concerned, the people of Virginia will be satisfied."

This shows a peculiar trait in the General. With all his dash and daring, both in war and peace, he was painfully shy. He loved hard work, but hated to be conspicuous.

Another quotation from the Financial Record for November 20th, 1886 follows:

"General Logan resumes his place as the leading counselor and guide of the system under very different auspices from those amid which he launched his speculative bark[10] four years ago. Then he came from an impoverished State and the only resources on which he could rely were those furnished by people comparatively poor. Today he is once again the master spirit, with the enormous wealth of the Standard Oil party at his command. Today the great value of the Danville system is everywhere appreciated. Under these conditions it is not a wild prophecy to make that a great advance in those stocks is yet to come; and better still, an advance which will be maintained."

November 22, 1886 was a big day in the New York stock exchange. The New York Times said: "Excitement ruled all day Saturday on the Stock Exchange. The opening hour witnessed such a scene as has seldom been known on any occasion other than a big panic. The public announcement of the big deal by which the control of the Richmond and Danville railroad was obtained by the Richmond and West Point Terminal Company had practically set the public crazy.

"All interest in Stock Exchange dealings centered in the Richmond Terminal pool. There was, when the hour for business came, a hurly-burly that seemed to have every broker of Wall Street in it. There was no opening price for the stock, or rather, there were a dozen opening prices, all different. At the same moment, in the same group of brokers, stock sold at 68 and at 76 in concert—the same stock that a month ago was neglected and sneered at as belonging to the cats and dogs contingent. The Stock Exchange has few incidents that may be quoted in comparison with

---

[10] Colloquial for a type of ship.

the project whose rapid execution has worked this wonder.

"As the day wore on there was somewhat of a subsidence in the excitement, but dealings continued active and spirited, and quotations remained stiff, with a tendency that seemed to lend color to the assertions of insiders that par was pretty sure to be reached soon. It is taken for granted that some important move will be made as soon as the Terminal's new management is fairly in power to develop and broaden the company's policy." (Quoted in Richmond Dispatch, November 23rd, 1886.)

But what was behind the sensational comeback? This is how it happened. The 1883 crash had occurred because the Southerners were lacking in capital. Shrewd manipulators supposedly headed by Jay Gould had used some of their old-time hocus-pocus to depress the Richmond and Danville and Terminal Company stock, shaking out Logan and his crowd who could no longer afford to hold on. But in spite of their cleverness these buyers did not realize the importance of their auxiliary Terminal holdings and proceeded to sell these off, as if they had no especial value.

The ousted Logan crowd, backed by Rockefeller and other capitalists, gradually bought up this Terminal stock, until they had the necessary control. The original owners realized that the Richmond and Danville Company could not prosper if separated from the Terminal Company. The question was whether the dog should wag the tail or the tail the dog! Now began a swift series of surprises for the Gould allies.[lxv]

Logan was now able to prove that several leases of the Richmond and Danville Company were illegally made and could not be perfected or amended without the consent of the Terminal Company—the leasing power of which he now controlled. The Southerners had thus stolen a march on their opponents. The Scott crowd recognized their own helplessness and acknowledged they were open for some proposition from the conquerors. In the end, the Logan party bought the entire stock of the Richmond and Danville, less some 5000 shares. The price paid was from 230 to 260 dollars per share. The Gould and Scott crowd were delighted to take their profits and retired from the scene of battle.

Logan came back in a very different situation from the one of four years before. In 1882-1883 he was backed by Southerners with very few resources. He had the Standard Oil Company behind him in 1886.

"The Hour" for November 27, 1886, sums up the new situation:

"There is no doubt that this great Southern Railway system, owning and controlling as it does some 2700 miles of railroad, going through the most fertile part of the South, must prove, if well managed, not only a paying road, but a well paying road. Somehow the eyes of the East and North are now turned to the development of the long neglected South. And it is but reasonable to hope, and indeed to believe, that the riches of the South will yield a richer harvest to investors than ever the West did. Anyhow, it seems that the capital of the North and East, as also of Europe, is going to try it. The Richmond Terminal and the Richmond and Danville systems have now been virtually absorbed by one syndicate, and the gentlemen who have undertaken this now successful work, are men of good standing and honor. Although the price of the 150,000 Terminal shares has risen from 35 to 76 in two weeks, yet it is after all only a bagatelle as compared with the ultimate results. If this rise would simply mean a clever stock operation, then of course the whole enterprise would end in a fiasco. But there is all the evidence that the main object of this reconstruction is based upon a solid and conservative basis, and the real proof will be that this terminal stock will not, like its predecessor five years ago, jump up to 260 one day and go to 75 the next. As long as the present holders of the stock beware of such pitfalls, all will be well with them. General T. M. Logan, whose somewhat checkered career in this railway system is strange and interesting, has once more come to the front as Vice-President. He has seen and felt the false power of speculation that once surrounded him. This gentleman was the originator of the Terminal system and, as usual, he was rewarded with the originator's and inventor's lot. In fact, he and his immediate friends were left to bear the brunt and loss some five years ago when the crash in Richmond and Danville and Richmond Terminal stock came. Of course, he not only lost his money, but was even ousted out of the Vice-Presidency of the road. Strange enough, he has now come before the public again, like a sort of railway Gustavus Vasa, to snatch the control from the very hands that deposed him. Let us hope General Logan has learnt, not only wisdom, but what is more, experience."

To celebrate his victory General Logan gave a party in New York. He invited all his friends who had lost in the Crash of 1883. Under each plate was a check in full for his loss. The authority for this is a letter from Lulu Logan Bentley. She quotes Mr. Joseph Bryan, one of General Logan's collaborators in the New York Railway affairs. Other associates in this work were Colonel A.S. Buford, James H. Dooley, J.B. Pace and E.D. Christian, all of Richmond.

The following is a summary of Railroad offices held by General Logan. Between the years of 1880 and 1892—Vice-President and Director of "Terminal" Company; in 1882-1883 and again in 1887, President of Virginia Midland Railway Company. This was in addition to his early Presidency of the Port Walthall Branch Railroad, and of course Vice-President of the Richmond and Danville Railroad.

General Logan sold the house at 14 West Franklin to Colonel A.S. Buford in 1886, when Katy was eighteen. He still had Algoma for the summers but he rented the Enders' home, opposite Dr. Hoge's Church on Fifth Street, between Franklin and Main for the winter (1886) of Katy's debut. Kate was in New York most of the fall at the Windsor Hotel, to be near her husband whose work kept him more and more in that city. While there, she arranged to have Katy's white debut dress made by Donovan, most famous New York couturier. It had five skirts of tulle and a top skirt of gauze striped in satin, trimmed with lilies of the valley. The pointed bodice was of watered silk with short puffed sleeves and of course, like all evening dresses of the period, it was buttoned up the back. Katy wore this to her first Monday German.

This most fashionable function of the year in Richmond was founded soon after the war. The dances then were called hops and all the music was furnished by a piano, a cello and a violin. The dances were given each week at the Spottswood Hotel on Main Street. After the hotel burned down in 1870 different Richmond people opened their houses for the hops. Next, these weekly Monday affairs were moved to St. Alban's Hall at the corner of Main and Third Street, or to Levy's Hall, formerly at Main and Eleventh Street. The balls also took place at Saenger Hall on Seventh near Marshall, Belvedere Hall, the Masonic Temple, the Jefferson Hotel and much later at the Commonwealth Club. The trouble between John B. Mordecai and Page McCarthy[sic] who fought a duel over the beautiful Miss Triplett was inaugurated at a St. Alban's Hall German. The cause of the duel was supposed to be that one of the men had written a poem about the Richmond belle:

"When Mary's queenly form I press

In Strauss' latest waltz,

I would as soon her lips caress

Although those lips be false."

For many years Jo Lane Stern (later General Stern) led the Richmond Monday German with great success.

A copy of the old invitations issued in 1877 shows that they were printed in script, not engraved. The officers at the time were as follows: Byrd Warwick, President; Charles Anderson, Vice President. The executive committee included Robert G. Cabell, Jr., G.A. Davenport, Alfred Gray, M.F. Montague, Charles P. Lathrop, Thomas Atkinson and R. D. Hudgins. The patronesses were: Mrs. H.T. Douglas, Mrs. J. Caskie Cabell, Mrs. O.A. Crenshaw, Mrs. John S. Wise, Mrs. John R. Triplett, Mrs. Bradley Johnston, and Mrs. J.S.D. Cullen.

In anticipation of Katy's debut ball an Italian dancing master spent two weeks drilling sixteen couples in the Fifth Street double parlors for the minuet. "Aunt Georgie," Mrs. William P. de Saussure, chaperoned and criticized the young people three times a week. Several beaux were buzzing around trying to secure Katy as a partner, but Mrs. Logan cut the Gordian knot by stating firmly, "Katy must dance with her uncle, Mr. de Saussure."

Richmond was in great excitement over the innovation of this proposed fancy dress ball, with the dancers having powdered hair and wearing Directoire costumes. Katy's dress was of red brocade with an overskirt of real silk lace, lent her by Mrs. John C. Calhoun. The Fifth Street house had large rooms on both sides, so after the minuet there was general dancing—lancers, waltzes, polkas and the still more lively gallop. How they managed the latter with long skirts no one can now imagine. But Mammy grumbled the next day at cleaning up great lengths of torn-off lace and satin.

A beautiful supper was furnished by the well-known colored caterer, John Dabney. Pyramids of iced nougat and other confections ornamented the supper table, with wines including Madeira from the Logan's South Carolina cellar.

During that same gay season John Dabney catered in a hurry for what was afterwards called "Mrs. Logan's Beauty Dinner."

One morning Kate was in the pantry arranging flowers when the butler handed her a telegram. "Meet Me Morning Train, T.M. Logan." Kate barely had time to send for Jim Conway's carriage and drive to the depot, arriving just as her husband stepped from the train.

The greetings were hurried, for the General had to catch another train almost at once for West Point and would not return until six p.m. He reminded Kate that she had promised a New York Railway man a dinner party with some of the prettiest girls of the city—and Richmond had always been famed for its beauties.

"Yes," said Kate. "But when?"

"Tonight—He's coming home with me then and we want a box at the theatre, too."

"But, General—" she gasped. The age of hast had not yet arrived and very few people even had telephones. "Well, I'll try. Even if there is no box left at the theatre I'll arrange for a dinner at eight."

Kate drove straight to the theatre but found all the boxes had been reserved. By then it was nearly noon.

Next she drove to John Dabney's house. Luckily, he was free for that evening but there was still the question of finding the necessary lavish supplies for it was after market hours.

"Well, Mrs. Logan, I have some things in my own ice box, and the fish and oyster places are never closed, so we may make out. You won't find too expensive because I'll mortify the price so it won't be too costive."

On her return home Mrs. Logan began first to consider whom she could invite. Katy, as usual, was equal to the occasion.

"We can't telephone," she said, "as so few people have those funny little contraptions. I'll run around the neighborhood and ask about seven. That'll be enough ladies—with you and me. We'll write notes for Ben to deliver to the men down town." Katy would not have dreamed of entering the business district without her father, or other escort.

The notes bore fine fruit, as all the men who accepted were entertaining and bright. They were Ran Tucker, Blair Bolling, Frank Williams, Eugene Massie. The Railway magnates from the North filled out the quota of men.

No wonder the escorts were happy and entertaining with such girls as May Handy, Rosalie Pleasants, Mary McCaw, Gertrude Rives and Emily Nolting near them. General Logan was right. Kate never failed him and "Mrs. Logan's Beauty Dinner" was now a crowning success.

But Kate's energetic planning, the clever men, and the lovely women would all have been in vain but for the supreme efforts of John Dabney!

Not so famous, but as much of a character as John Dabney in a different way, was the livery man,

James Conway. He was a grizzled darky who drove his own neat closed carriage. He lived mostly by working for the Logans. His stable was nearby and it was almost as convenient to reach him as if he had had a telephone. He was a great friend of Mammy's and adored the children. Lilybud was for him "Miss Lily Bugs," and he presented this surname to the other little girls, who became Miss Meta "Bugs" and Miss Lena "Bugs." The children loved to ride in his roomy carriage lined in heavy button-tufted red satin. It was drawn by two sleek black horses. The smaller girls called them "Fancy—and Fury" as if they were one double animal, but Meta loved each one separately and would not agree that they looked alike because, she said, "Their expressions are so different!"

James Conway also enjoyed having the children with him. He would be offended if the Logans failed to call him for several days. He would arrive at the kitchen door and insist to Mammy that he had seen one of the children looking pale and only a drive would cure her.

Katy always had James Conway drive her to parties. The General thought it very out of place an escort to pay for a debutante's carriage.

One cold night in 1883 the family had gone to Howardsville. The dark loneliness of the country station terrified the smaller sisters. On top of that came their first experience in a rough surrey and over muddy country roads.

"We want Jim Conway's carriage! We want Jim Conway's carriage and the nice city streets," they halfsang, half wept together all the way up the jolting hill. Lilybud and Lena did everything together. They dressed alike and had all their clothes in common, for Lily was older, but Lena was larger for her age. They were always called Lilybud-and-Lena in one word. Although they looked so different, no one really knew them apart. Often they confused their own identities, not knowing who had said or even thought a particular thing. Lena's mashed finger became Lilybud's pain. Lily's sore throat made Lena choke. They both adored their sister Katy and loved to see her dress up in her new clothes.

That same autumn, on the way back from New York, Katy visited in Louisville and Colonel Mason Brown, who married one of the famous Preston sisters, gave her a dinner of twenty covers. Her gown for the occasion was made by the New York Miss Borgas, who was Mrs. Grover Cleveland's dressmaker. Mrs. Cleveland had permitted the copying of one of her evening dresses for Katy who had taken the finished skirt from New York to Richmond. The dinner was on Saturday and on Thursday the waist had not arrived! Katy telegraphed her father: "SEND THE BODY AT ONCE," which caused much amusement, especially to the General who loved family jokes.

One incident which brought down the house did not make the General laugh. The younger Richmond set were having a benefit play in the Logan's front parlor. The audience was in the back room and the folding doors between acted as a curtain. Katy was the haughty heroine, her swain being handsome, dignified Mr. John Rutherfoord. He bent on one knee and seizing her hand, gasped: "I a-dore you."

Katy airily tossed aside his rejected hand and started majestically toward the wings with every fringed blue satin flounce bristling with arrogance. But instead of the tense silence she had expected to greet her dramatic exit, a loud laugh burst from the audience. Mammy rushed from the wings to the stage. She stooped to pick up something. Involuntarily Katy turned to look . . . Oh, horror, there in her wake was her blue satin bustle! The success of the evening was assured, but Mully's innate refinement was offended and he never wished this play referred to again.

In spite of his shyness, the General loved gaiety and entertaining in his own, but he had never changed his ideas about not going to entertainments in other people's houses.

That same winter of 1886 Martha Snead of Louisville visited Katy in Richmond. Mrs. Logan was in New York and so the eldest daughter kept house. She decided to have oyster suppers every night after sledding parties, for this was a snowy winter. The young people loved to slide down the steep hill from Fifth to Franklin. Great was Kate's surprise on her return home to learn that her daughter had had a party every single night! These entertainments were full of fun and everybody enjoyed them, especially Katy who loved to see others happy. She herself had always been on the go, ever since she began to toddle at only nine months of age. But she stuck to her rules against round dancing. She had plenty of invitations and bushels of favors, but she still sat out the waltzes with her partners, joining only in the figure dances. She had numerous admirers and loved to share them with others who might otherwise have been neglected.

If less popular girls decorated the walls she could not be happy on the floor. The former wallflowers never seemed to guess whence came their unexpected popularity. Strange to say, the courteous beaux of that day did not object to Katy's management. But when the parties were given in the Logan home there was one person who especially appreciated Katy's maneuvres to make others happy—her father.

Of course General Logan was no longer the slim young man of the sixties but his cheeks were as rosy as ever, his eyes the same clear, twinkling blue, and his head was still covered with a thick growth of dark brown hair. For years had had worn a moustache and his square-cut, slightly wavy beard almost concealed the usual wing collar of the period.

In the early 1880's Kate's sweet, unwrinkled face was almost as youthful as when Mully had first known her. Her complexion was like one of her own roses, but her soft hair was as white as snow—like a silver crown. This snowy hair, piled high, and with a wavy pompadour, gave her great dignity, in spite of her extreme animation. Katy's beaux always asked for Mrs. Logan and loved to converse with her—or rather to listen to her accounts of the old days, before and during the War. She never hesitated for the right word as her golden voice went on and on.

Chapter XIV

Sunday in Richmond
1887

On a winter Sunday morning in 1887, Mammy started to dress the children for Church. In those days in Richmond everybody went to Sunday services. The Logan's Church was St. Paul's at the corner of Grace and Ninth.

A moment later the two little girls were sheathed in exactly similar green coats. All that showed were their feet and a bit of earless face, for their Kate Greenaway bonnets came down over their heads and were tied with ribbon bows beneath their chins. Their hands were completely lost in little muffs of cloth and fur. Lilybud said she felt like a worm in a cocoon, especially as two little fur ears stood up in front of her bonnet like the feelers on the caterpillar in her favorite Alice in Wonderland.

Their mother's cocoon was of sealskin with a cap to match. The fur hat was surmounted by a large winged bow, like a bird about to fly away. Where the coat ended, her dark skirt was looped up on the sides and had a bustle in the back. In those days women felt as immodest without a bustle as girls of today would minus lipstick. Meta wore a bustle, as she was mature for her age. She was even more beautiful than she had been as a baby.

Katy was in New Orleans visiting Uncle Sam and Aunt Virginia, and Jimmy was away at school. That left only the three youngest children to accompany their parents to Church.

Soon they were walking down the few blocks from Fifth near Main to Ninth and Grace. The General went on ahead holding Lena by the hand. He too was cocooned in a long overcoat, but the winter sunlight glistened on his white collar and heightened the glow on his ruddy cheeks. His bright blue eyes shone with love and understanding whenever he bent his head to talk to his little daughter.

In a few minutes they had reached the Church. St. Paul's beloved rector, the Reverend Charles F.E. Minnegerode, had been in charge there for thirty years. His church had had many distinguished guests. On October 7th, 1860 "Baron Renfrew,"[11] the Prince of Wales, later King Edward VII, came to service at St. Paul's. Dr. Minnegerode's sermon that day was (ironically, some thought) from the text, "That ye may be blameless in the day of our Lord." As the royal party left the church, the organist played "God Save the Queen."

---

[11] One of the lesser known titles for the heir apparent to the British throne.-Ed.

Dr. Minnegerode used to say to his organist, Jacob Reinhardt, "You get the crowd, Jake, and I'll preach to it." Whatever the reason, the church usually thronged. Dr. Minnegerode had even been able to attract many to his early Lenten services. With the rising sun shining through the east windows of the church, he once remarked: "Why doesn't my whole congregation attend these services? If the sun can rise, so can you."

As is usual in such cases, this remark was heard by those present but was aimed at the very ones whom it could not reach—the absent. Anyway, it bore fruit, for the early services became a part of Richmond's social life and invitations to breakfast after church were the style. This was in the early days of his pastorate. But St. Paul's continued to draw crowds at the regular services, and midday dinner invitations became general. A row of young men, like stags at a ball, stood on the Grace Street pavement at the close of the services to escort the young ladies to their homes.

Everybody stopped General and Mrs. Logan to ask about Miss Katy. Was she having a good time? When would she return? Katy's beaux looked quite disconsolate as the other young men started off with their chosen girls. The whole procession then made its way over to Franklin Street.

There will never again be any street as glamorous as Richmond's old Franklin—the Via Sacra. Fifth Avenue's Easter show pales into insignificance besides those noon Sunday parades from St. Paul's church up Franklin as far as Monroe Park. From their windows the stay-at-homes watched the passing by of Richmond beauties. There were May Handy with her Parma violets, Mary McCaw, Cyane Williams, Elise Strother, Anna Boykin, Frances Scott, Elise Williams, Bessie Lay, Florine Nolting, and Amelie Rives, later Princess Troubetskoy[12].

A few months later (April, 1888) this same lovely Amelie Rives was to turn Richmond upside down by her publication of "The Quick or the Dead?" The Logan children were not allowed to read this sensational novel. They could not understand why. Nor can we of today understand why there should have been a ban on Amelie's first book.

All Richmond girls were charming. They knew what to say and how to say it. To judge by the expression on the men's faces, the debutantes were making themselves unusually fascinating today. Whether their talk was aspiring or not, their hats were certainly pointing skyward. Most of these sat up like junior stovepipes, and as if that were not high enough, on the top of the pipe was an extra tier of fur, ribbon or feathers.

A large proportion of the men's faces were handsomely trimmed in moustaches, which were the horror of Lilybud and Lena. In those days it was considered a mark of indifference and neglect on the part of a beau not to try to kiss the younger sisters. The children's instinct reacted and save them often from these embraces. They could sense a moustache quite a distance away and before the message was

---

[12] Amelie Rives, a Southern novelist, would marry a Russian aristocrat, Pierre Troubetskoy and scandalized Richmond society with her erotic writings and personal life.-Ed.

telegraphed to their eyes their legs had started them in the opposite direction.

General and Mrs. Logan and the children were turning now in the other direction from the St. Paul's throng. Kate as usual had an errand of mercy on the North side of Richmond. As they approached Twelfth and Marshall they passed another crowd of Episcopal Church worshippers from Monumental Church.

"Why is it called that?" asked Meta. "It's round at the top and has no steeple like our own St. Paul's."

"Oh, I thought you knew," answered her father as they strolled along. "That's where the Richmond theatre used to stand. In 1811 just a year after it was built, it was the scene of a terrible tragedy!"

"What kind of a tragedy?" asked Meta. The smaller girls stopped skipping and crowded around her. "What's a tragedy?"

"Something very bad, dearest. This time it was a fire!"

"Did the theatre all burn down or up or something?"

"Every way possible. During the second act of 'Raymond and Agnes,' flames began to rage behind the scenes."

"Was de peoples all bu'nt up, like logs o' wood?" Lena asked with intense interest.

"Not all, but at least seventy-two were destroyed. Among those lost were the Governor of Virginia, George Smith. Every home in Richmond was grief stricken. Members of the United States Senate wore badges of mourning and for four months no festivities were permitted in Richmond. Later it was decided to place a church on the site, as a memorial to the victims."

In regard to this memorial Monumental Church, Mrs. Logan wrote later in her Memoirs: "Many years after the War there came to Richmond, Virginia, a man very lame and so like Booth that everyone remarked on the resemblance. He became the rector at Monumental Church and drew large crowds by his brilliant oratory. After he had lived there some time he had a Shakespeare class, being wonderful in his capacity as reader and teacher. He went from Richmond to Atlanta. After years of clerical life, his career ended disastrously. I have often heard his name coupled with that of Booth and after his defection there was a rumor, believed by many, that he was none other than Booth himself, who had made his escape when pursued, after Lincoln's death, notwithstanding his broken leg. His general likeness to Booth, his extreme lameness, his great histrionic talent and thorough acquaintance with Shakespeare all pointed to the fact that he was the escaped assassin of Lincoln. The sequel also gave the story more credit-his relapse into dissipation, when he was no longer able to keep up his feigned character.[13] The elder Booth would never act in Washington after the great tragedy."

---

[13] Again, as with above, there were a multitude of rumors and stories about Booth's escape or that an impersonator had been killed instead of him at Garrett's Farm. This story, like others, is implausible in several regards, notably for the fact that Booth was a widely recognized actor of his time and his public presence in Richmond no less would certainly have garnered more attention.-Ed.

Pursuing the fascinating subject, Mrs. Logan gives another incident: "One of our best scouts, later the Reverend Frank Stringfellow, an Episcopal minister, gave me a most interesting account of why Booth killed Lincoln. There was, in prison at the North, a great friend of Booth's, a Southerner, by name Bell, I think, who was court-martialed. This friend wrote Booth that such was the case; and that there would be no hope for him were he court-martialed, and that his only chance was to have a judicial trial, for he was not guilty; and as Booth was a friend of Lincoln he might have some influence in procuring justice for Bell.

Booth saw Lincoln and stated the case, saying that his friend wished only a fair trial. Lincoln promised to look into it at once. In the meantime, Bell indicated his great uneasiness to Booth, asking if he had done anything. Booth went again to Lincoln, who once more promised to intercede. Finally, Bell telegraphed that nothing had been done and begged Booth to try again. Lincoln again promised to do his best, which meant of course justice to the prisoner, but on that day Bell was court-martialed and shot. However the fault or mistake was made, Booth resented it as something personal and felt that he had been trifled with. Smarting under the insult, as he deemed it, besides being deeply distressed over the fate of his friend, he determined to do the fearful deed. I think he was temporarily insane.[14]"

Mrs. Logan's assertion that the supposed Booth went later to Atlanta fits in nicely with a letter from Mrs. Henry P. Thompson, a descendant of Sarah Edwina Booth, who was sister to Julius Brutus Booth, father of Edwin and John Wilkes Booth. I quote the letter:

"One of the events of my girlhood when Edwin Booth was filling an engagement in our town (Atlanta) were the visits he made to our home. He, my grandfather, William Booth Walker of Georgia, (Commissary General of Confederate Troops) and John Wilkes Booth (who under an assumed name was Rector of a church in Atlanta) used to spend the nights after the plays in my grandfather's room

---

[14] It is unclear where this unique story originated; there is nothing in the historical record to verify it. Frank Stringfellow had been one of Col. John S. Mosby's scouts. However, this myth seems more of a revisionist account designed to shift blame away from the Southern Cause, of which Booth was a dedicated follower, and frame the murder as more of a personal vendetta than a political assassination. This would conveniently place some of the blame with Lincoln. Lincoln and Booth never met; repeated meetings as described almost certainly would have been documented or witnessed at some point. The only other time the two were in close proximity was when Lincoln attended a play with Booth in it and when Booth attended, uninvited, the Second Inaugural Ball. Also, it is unlikely that a prisoner incarcerated in a Federal prison camp would have ready access to a telegraph office.-Ed.

in our house. At the dinner table all three entered into the general table talk, but the late hours of the nights they spent alone. The Rector often gave readings from Hamlet, King Lear and Othello to raise funds for his Church. His daughter, Miriam Booth A. went to England and was an accomplished actress, portraying Shakespearean roles. My grandfather was always loyal to John Wilkes Booth in his assumed roles, but we children did not know of his real identity until after his death. This is supposed to have taken place from an overdose of chloral in Dallas, Texas.

Florence W. Thompson,
January 22, 1932

Another interesting point made by Mrs. Thompson, was that her "cousin" could easily have been the mummy referred to in Time, December 28, 1931, because he went westward from Atlanta and the man referred to in Time killed himself in Enid, Oklahoma about twenty-nine years ago.

Chapter XV

Telautograph and
Katy's Wedding
1888

G eneral Logan's fancy for "contraptions",
as he called them, was fast bringing him
to another turning point in his life. The
locomotive, the telegraph, the telephone, even the
newer phonograph were beginning to pall. Besides, he
loved promoting and was looking for some new work
where he could combine his interest in inventions
with the promotion of something worth while.

At this juncture he was introduced to Professor
Elisha Gray, one of the many who claimed to have
preceded Bell with the telephone. However that may
be, Gray's new invention was certainly fascinating.
Instead of allowing two people to converse from afar,
it reproduced writing or pictures at a distance, as
indicated by its name—Telautograph. Other types of
such a machine had been invented before,[lxvi] but in

these earlier kinds the paper on the transmitter was constantly moving and it required great skill to write legibly. Operation was further handicapped because there was no provision for lifting the pen, and the figures blurred and ran together.

Gray's was the first telautograph to overcome these defects. General Logan, convinced of the value of the invention, and, over the protests of Kate, agreed to promote it. In this way the Gray National Telautograph Company was organized under the laws of Virginia in 1888 with an authorized capital of $15,000,000, of which $6,000,000 was issued to Professor Elisha Gray and his associates for the purchase of certain patents he had applied for and received, covering the first telautograph. General Logan was made President.

The children were delighted when two test machines were set up in their home and they could write from room to room. You wrote on the transmitter and it came out on the receiver.

Their city residence was now at 500 West Franklin, a large brick house facing the street close in front like a fortress. It was not particularly attractive. Since the War the architecture in Richmond had needed the hand of some of the Virginia County squires, like Thomas Jefferson or General Cocke of Bremo. The "brown-stone" craze and the various Victorian types had hit the city in full force. The most stupendous architectural atrocity was the projected new City Hall, not to be finished until 1893. The beautiful original building had been torn down in error. The collapse of the Capitol floor in 1870 had frightened the city fathers into fearing that all public buildings were unsafe. Four years later they had incontinently razed the beautiful Greek style City Hall, Doric columns and all. When it was too late and the place was more than half destroyed they discovered on reaching the inner structure that the edifice was particularly strong and built for permanence.

But Richmond was slowly learning her lesson and the houses going up in the westward extension of the city were improving daily in style.

The children were not interested in architecture, but they delighted in the lovely grounds of their new home. There they could play to their hearts' content such games as Puss in the Corner and Hide and Seek.

Among Lilybud's and Lena's playmates at this time were the Langhornes, Nannie, afterward Lady Astor[15], and their smaller brother "Buck". They lived not far from the Logans on West Grace Street and were a joy to the neighborhood because of their buoyant spirits and ready wit. It was always exciting to visit the Langhornes, as their house was full of happy hurley-burley, with the lovely sweet-natured Mrs. Langhorne going serenely on her way, which was always the right way. The children go their sprightliness from their father, Mr. "Chilly" Langhorne,

---

[15] Nancy Langhorne Astor, a native Virginian, after marrying Waldorf Astor, successfully ran for her husband's open seat in Parliament in 1919 after he was elevated to the House of Lords. She was the first woman to be a Member of Parliament in the House of Commons. Of note, her first husband was Robert Gould Shaw II, a cousin of Colonel Robert Shaw, commander of the 54th Massachusetts Infantry, comprised of African American soldiers during the War.-Ed.

the best raconteur in the Virginia of that day. It was fun to run into him, as he always said something to make you laugh. His son, Buck, was just the same way later—the most popular person in the state.

But best of all it was to catch a sight of the second eldest sister, Irene, afterwards Mrs. Charles Dana Gibson. She was not yet grown but was already one of the queens of the Richmond Beauty Parade. Naturally, she had a constant stream of beaux fluttering around her. A great friend of her early youth was the brilliant young Nicholas Longworth of Cincinnati, later Speaker of the House of Representatives. His name does not appear in the Guest Book of the Logan's country home, Algoma, as does that of another of Irene's beaux, Mr. Legh Page of Richmond.

The rather trying styles of the day put no damper on Irene's beauty. The more unbecoming the style, the more beautiful did she appear. One who saw her in those days has a vivid memory of her tall, majestic figure, brilliant coloring, bright blue eyes and sparkling animation. No wonder the artist, Charles Dana Gibson, fell in love with her and used her as his inspiration for the Gibson girl!

Little did the Logan children realize, when they delighted to play with the "tom-boy" Nannie Langhorne that she would someday be Lady Astor—the first woman member of Parliament. Still less would anyone have expected to see her become severe and strict in her notions of what a young person should be and do. In those early days, she was always the leader in pranks and mischief. Her next younger sister, Phyllis, was much more staid and quiet in her ways. They were different in looks, but equally lovely, as was proved later on when the whole tribe was known as "the beautiful Langhorne sisters."

Another lively friend was Ellie Carmichael. Her father, the Reverend Hartley Carmichael, took the place of Dr. Minnegerode when he resigned his pastorate at St. Paul's because of old age and ill health. He was a brilliant preacher, writer, musician, and very handsome to boot.

Ellie Carmichael and Buck Langhorne loved to drive around in Buck's little go-cart and also to hitch their sleds and wagons to other people's sleighs and carriages. They were a team for mischief! The Logans were not permitted to do delightful things like hitching on to other people's vehicles, but were forced to take their fun demurely, driving their small dog cart drawn by the fat grey pony, Hippo. The Logans were not allowed on the street alone. This was a great offense to their dignity and caused much teasing from the other lively youngsters.

Mammy knew that teasing hurt, so she finally agreed to follow the children, but on the other side of the street. She was careful not to call to them across the barrier. It was always very exciting to go to the Langhorne's, with or without Mammy, because one hoped for a glimpse of the elder sister Irene.

Lilybud and Lena had a governess, whom they adored, Miss Annie Hobson. But they always felt a little apologetic, because they did not go out to school like the others. Children hate to be different!

The children's most frequent playmates were their cousins, "Seppie" and William deSaussure. Their mother had been Georgie Logan and their father,

William deSaussure, a Charlestonian, was an attorney and worked for the General.

The deSaussures dined every Sunday with the Logans. This was a great time for, using the whole house as a playground, to the horror of Mammy, they turned all her week-end neatness into a grand mess. "Look what you done did to my beds!" she would exclaim, calling for Emma, the maid, to come and repair the damage.

The Logan children liked the roomy Franklin Street house with its modern inventions of steam heat and electric light. It was fun to snap on the carbon bulbs instead of looking for a match.

The front and back parlors were even larger that the Fifth Street ones. The hospitable dining-room was just to the rear, and on the other side was the study where the General worked. It had a window on the street from which the children could look out at the busy traffic. This bay window was better than a theatre box for watching the Sunday procession and finding out which girls had caught new beaux.

To the children, the grown people these days were rather uninteresting, as all they could talk about was politics and then more politics. It seemed a large man named Cleveland had been President for four years and he wanted the post again, though the young people could not see why as there were ever so many mean things said about the President in some of the New York papers which the General was always buying. The children would hear the newsboy outside shrieking, "New York papers!" and then they knew their father would be rapping on the window and calling the boy to the door. They never could see why the General was more interested in this vendor than in the exciting man who called musically from his wagon: "Wa-a-eter millions, waaater millions, fresh and fine, jes' from de vine, green rind, red meat, fulla juice and so-o-o sweet."

You could eat water melon—yum-yum, but what could you do with a newspaper except use it to light a fire?

On a summer day Lilybud and Lena were looking for another man in a wagon marked "Kennebec River Ice". As the ice-cart rounded the corner Uncle Ben beckoned the driver to the back door. The children rushed to meet him. He was such a nice fellow because he always gave Lilybud and Lena delicious slivers of his product. It seemed so mysterious to think of that ice having been cut last winter away up in Maine and now being used in Virginia! When the children went in the house again the elders were still talking about the election in November and whether Harrison or Cleveland would be chosen. It seemed that when Cleveland was elected four years before he had been the first Democrat since Lincoln and the Southerners set great store by that fact.

Politics was not so interesting to the children as the news that their eldest sister was engaged to Dr. Bruns of New Orleans and would be married in October.

Most of the summer of 1888 the family spent at Algoma. This place was a land of enchantment with its rolling hills, its mysterious woods and its many streams for fishing. To the children the house also looked beautiful. They adored the gingerbread concoction designed by the Italian Caracristi. Above all, they loved the little cupola. From there they could look out in all directions. On the South and West the plantation hills started a ridge which increased in height, tier on tier, ending in the far distant Blue Ridge. The rest of the horizon was defined by the "big" woods which went back for miles into Buckingham Country.

The only trouble with Algoma was that Lilybud and Lena saw very little of their mother, who was far busier at the farm than she had been in the city. Kate's main occupation all her life was helping other people. She was forever packing baskets or taking dainties from her own kitchen and clothes from her own wardrobe for whomever came along and asked her for them. Once she nearly had pneumonia from giving away all her winter underwear. It took several days to order more from Richmond. Her idea was: "You had better give to ten unworthy applicants than to let a single worthy person go hungry for either food or sympathy."

Mully was just as tender-hearted but not so feudalistic. He did not believe in pauperizing and was always trying to invent new ways of making work in order to keep his end of the county humming with employment. Kate could never get over the idea that all of Mully's "made" work was an extravagance, costing so much more that simple charity. They had many good-humored arguments on the subject of the proper methods of helping the county, whether by direct or indirect relief.

Kate would rummage around during her husband's absences and give away most of his cherished old shoes and jackets, and in this Meta was much like her mother. Lilybud and Lena never knew when their favorite shoes and hats would disappear.

Meta and the General both adored horses, and on one occasion the General took advantage of his wife's absence to buy a Mr. Carrington's horses and a good pack of fox-hounds from North Carolina. This Kate called a needless expense. "Each person has his own idea of extravagance and economy," thought Mully, "and each one's idea is different from his neighbor's or his wife's!"

But Kate fancied that she might have planned a great many better uses for that money than to exchange it for a stable full of horses and a kennel full of dogs. The only son, Jimmy, loved the hounds and took excellent care of them. He always had a procession of pups dogging his footsteps.

One morning at four the General rode off to a hunt on Katy's horse, leaving word for his daughter to follow on Flora, an old reliable but no jumper. Later, Katy, wearing her beaver hat, started alone and finally came up with the hunters in a big field back of Miss Bell Irving's. "Job" Trotter saw her and made her leave her hat in a cabin and wear his cap, for they were going through brush and briar. Mully jumped a blind ditch and down he went, and Katy nearly on top of him. They changed horses and Faerie carried Katy faithfully over all the other ditches. Ran Tucker climbed off old Stella and went to sleep under a tree where the others found him about ten o'clock, on the way home. But Kate heard about Mully's spill and made him promise never to jump again.

Woe to late risers at Algoma! About six o'clock every morning the General's voice would ring all over the house: "Come on fellows, the horses are waiting. It's time to start!" He hated to know others were asleep while he was awake. In all other respects he was more than considerate and gentle.

Once, hearing a great fracas, he went into the next room and found knick-knacks of the day strewn all over the place. The rather stormy Meta had been using violent methods with her gentler brother Jimmy. The General entered the room, stumbling over bric-a-brac, and trying to look severe. "Fellows," he began, vainly attempting to give a harsh note to his soft Carolinian voice, "Fellows," —then explosively—his bright blue eyes twinkling with fun— "Consider yourselves scolded!" his first and last attempt at home discipline.

On October 17, 1888, the General's oldest child, Katy, was married at Algoma to Dr. Henry Dickson Bruns.[lxvii] And what festivity attended the wedding! Thirty-seven people stayed at Algoma all week, and fifty were there over the week-end. John Dabney, who had superintended Katy's debut party, was caterer for her wedding. The whole affair became famous as an example of Southern hospitality.

Katy wore a pinkish cream grosgrain silk with a tulle veil caught up into a cap and surmounted by a bunch of lilies of the valley. The same flowers circled her neck, caught up her skirt here and there, and in more real but less permanent form, composed her bridal bouquet. She wore a pointed basque and the heavy material of her dress was gathered up in the back to simulate a bustle.

There were eight bridesmaids and many guests. Dr. Minnegerode of St. Paul's church performed the ceremony. The festivities were enjoyed by all except Lily, who was so grieved to lose her eldest sister that she retired behind the parlor sofa and sobbed to her heart's content, for the music and laughter drowned the sound of her weeping. What would Algoma be without Katy? How she hated those people who were taking her off to New Orleans! She included in this antipathy not only Dr. Bruns, but his two aunts, the Misses Dickson. Unable to bear the sounds of merriment around her, she stole away from her hiding place and retired to her own small desk where she wrote through her tears:

> "So they all went away
>
> With very little fixin'
>
> Katy, Dr. Bruns and
>
> The Misses Dickson."

She was offended when the guests laughed at this effusion. She stole away to find the most understanding one of all—her father. He comforted her as far as he could, considering her loss was also his own.

But he had done his best to give the bridal party of four a happy send-off. He had lent them a private car from his Railroad.

After the bridal couple had driven off to the station amid loud huzzas and the throwing of many shoes, the guests and family started an old-fashioned quadrille— "Up the middle and down again." There were many to participate, for people had driven to the wedding from miles and miles away. The Virginians of those days could certainly cover distances. They not only covered space in buggies and surreys but also on the ballroom floor.

The leader called, "Get your partners!" waving his arms in a large inclusive gesture. Joe Stinson gave his fiddle a preliminary scrape and the guitars and banjos followed after. "Oh, for the days of Kerry dancing!" With the two long lines of partners now facing each other, the director's voice again boomed out the command: "Up the middle and down again! Promenade all!" This was followed by the hollow-square formation of a dos-á-dos and a coquettish rendition of Peek-a-Boo, the leader skillfully directing a grand chain, the Binding of the Sheaves. By some unknown magic Mr. Stinson, from an ordinary instrument and a paltry melody, could wring celestial music. His favorite was "The Ship That Never Returned."

As soon as the wedding day was over the grownups reverted again to politics. Who would win, Cleveland or Harrison? Elections came and went. And oh, sad days for the Democrats—Harrison had won!

Chapter XVI

A Day At Algoma
1890

Harrison's Republican victory upset most of all the old butler, Uncle Davy, who had "fit" through the war with his young master, one of the Rives family. He spoke his mind to Mammy: "I heah dey done put one o' dem triflin' Yankees back to oversee us in Washington. If dey really need a President what am a President, why don' dey send down here for our General Logan?"

Life at Algoma seemed to go on just the same as ever with Harrison in the saddle. The daily horseback rides were taken for granted. One morning in May, General Logan appeared at the porte cochere in his familiar corduroys with a visor cap to match, and high black riding boots. He did not approve of the Virginian custom of wearing cast-off city clothes in the country. His army training had taught him that special togs were appropriate to special activities. But the girls were more independent. They came out of the house this morning in white shirtwaists with dark wool riding skirts made for the side saddle. They would have broken their necks trying to get about in this costume if there had not been a loop in the middle of the longest part which fastened to a button just below the waist.

The sun was considered injurious to the complexion, so each child was furnished with a bonnet, now dangling by its strings. These were not regular sunbonnets. They had stiffly starched white piquet visors lined in pink and ruffled along the edge and they did not come down over the ears. The backs were of very full muslin gathered with a drawstring at the nape of the neck.

Both little girls wore their straight bangs almost to the eyebrows. Their back hair hung down in large corkscrew curls. These were Mammy's delight and the young people's horror. Only men, boys and eccentrics wore their hair bobbed in those days. Lily's hair was dark brown and Lena's light chestnut. Both children had grey-blue eyes but Lena's face was round and rosy, while Lily's was narrow and old-fashioned.

In a few minutes up came Wyatt with two horses, followed by the stable boy, Ben, leading a third. First up to the porch, inside the porte cochere, came the General's large grey, Gladstone. The grey was restive but the former cavalry officer was too quick for him and had mounted before the horse even knew what was happening. Gladstone hated to wait and began curvetting around as soon as he reached the open road. The General held him skillfully in check until the girls had joined him in the drive. They were mounted on the large bay carriage horses, Flora and Stella.

Off they started, but not very fast because the General was always interested in everything he saw along the way. Up the road a little piece the cavalcade came upon Uncle Morris unloading his ox-cart. The General stopped to direct the dumping of the crushable red stone at just the proper places.

The children were delighted to find that, as usual, black Morris Radford and his red and white oxen understood each other perfectly. The old man didn't use sharp, clipped directions, but talked to the beasts almost without inflection, so that they obeyed not the tones but the very words. "Jest a leddle furder—now, dat'll do. All right." Strangely enough the oxen obeyed him. The children were delighted and began to talk to the oxen themselves, but for all the beasts cared, their voices might have come from the birds in the budding trees.

Morris had been brought up on a diet of fish, for his mother, Sophie, angled from morning to night, slowly following the creeks as they wound in and out toward the river. No matter how early it was her string already glistened with scaly victims.

Morris loved to tell about the only time his mother had ever hurried. Progress had come up the James River, for the Kanawha Canal rights had been bought by the Chesapeake and Ohio Railroad. One day in April, 1881, a crowd assembled near Howardsville to see the first engine arrive on the newly laid tracks.

Talk and plans of railroads and engines had not penetrated Sophie Radford's mind—taken up, as always, by her dreams of angling. This morning, Sophie's crop of worms was especially succulent and the fish unusually greedy. She was squatting near the mouth of her favorite creek and about to draw out a glistening bass. Suddenly she heard a terrific noise, looked up from her line and saw—the advancing locomotive. It seemed to her a frightful black monster swooping down to gobble her up just as she had expected later to gobble up the poor fish. Sophie dropped her fish and line and, for the first and last time in her leisurely life, she "took out and ran."

She was about to race past a workman ploughing in the low grounds, but he caught her arm and pulled her to a stop. "What's the matter, Aunt Sophie? Where's your line and fish? What's your hurry?"

As soon as she could get her breath she explained: "Law's sakes, I 'bleeged to hurry. Ain't I done seed him chargin' up de river—de ole Devil hisself a-puffin and blowin' and smokin' he pipe!" No one could ever induce Aunt Sophie to ride on a train!

By the time they had heard all this again from Morris the horses had grown restless so the three galloped off down the long lane and took the road around the farm, stopping for a chat with old man Cambridge Mosely, who was limping pitifully.

"Why are you limping?" asked the General. "Didn't you hurt your arm, not your foot?"

"'Scuse me, Gen'al, how folks gwine know I'se got a misery, cep'n I limp?"

The General laughed good naturedly. "Here take this dollar and buy yourself something to cure your misery, wherever it is!"

From the joy on the old man's face even the children guessed the nature of the balm he was going to buy.

As they continued down the ribbon of red road, winding through a dell of thick woods, pied with delicate blooms—bloodroot, hepatica, wild geranium, and innocence, blue-eyed as though fallen from the sky—Lilybud and Lena gravely listened to their father discoursing on one of his pet topics:

"Illness and death you cannot prevent, little fellows, but remember, most of our troubles are manmade. Do your best to make these unnecessary troubles vanish, as they surely will one day when we have an unselfish world!" He lapsed into silence and then said: "Avoid unkind words in particular."

The children were old enough to realize that his emphasis on this was justified. Never cross himself, he could not tolerate rudeness in others.

"Why deliberately increase the sum of human pain by unkindness?" he went on half to himself.

When they had left Mosely far behind, the General again urged his horse into a gallop. "Hurry, funny fellows, we're off to the low grounds."

Soon they came upon the overseer, Mr. Stinson, mounted on his old white horse, Dolly. The children, always seeing him on horseback, considered him the original centaur, for man and beast seemed a part of each other.

While Mr. Stinson and the General were in conference about crops, the children were fascinated by the slow arching flight of large naked-faced birds around the half dead trees of "Buzzard's Roost." Nearer at hand, they heard the water thrushes singing in the willows and alders along the creekside, while the children sniffed with delight the sweetness of honeysuckle.

Mr. Stinson pointed vigorously to this very creek side. "But, General, those bushes draw up the earth from the crops—they ought to be cut, like I said before."

Now the children listened eagerly. They loved this old argument. For once the General was firm. Accustomed to the luxuriant growth of the Carolinas he refused to have his roadside bushes and climbers hacked away because they "drew the ground." Mr. Stinson called honeysuckle, snowberries, and the rest, "weeds."

The General called them "hedgerows" and explained how lucky they were in Virginia to have such volunteers as dogwood, red-bud, mountain laurel and honeysuckle. Why even Mrs. Trollope, who started the British fashion of making the pot boil by abusing America, had turned around in her tracks and raved about the Blue Ridge Section with its beautiful natural growth! All of this the General explained to his daughters.

General Logan loved the way the scrub pines and cedars sprang up unbidden everywhere, giving this half-mountainous part of the country an all-year-round greenness. He used to say that even bare branches, etched against the sky, had a beauty all their own and that many trees, which look most alive in summer, need winter to bring out their individuality. To him trees had personality, being the most permanent of living things, outlasting flowers, animals and people. It hurt him to see one destroyed after all the years it had taken to develop. So, instead of cutting down and tearing up, his idea was to put in more and more trees and shrubs. And in this planting, he was very successful.

"Tree tops are inspiring," he explained, "but roots are like the Biblical sinners—they love darkness rather than light. Therefore don't leave the dug-up rootlets exposed to sun rays, but see that they are blanketed with their own earth and with sacking, and pack them down properly, so that they'll feel at home. Especially, don't starve them afterwards. Plants must eat and drink as we do. What you need here as elsewhere is old-fashioned gumption." The General loved that word gumption. His own large supply must have helped him greatly in his skirmishes during the sixties!

On reaching home after their ride, the father and daughters went into the dining-room. They were a little late, so everyone else had left the breakfast table.

"Where is mother?" they asked.

"She done gone in de rose garden," Davey explained. Then he hobbled out to the pantry and brought in steaming trays with scrambled eggs, bacon, and piles of crisp, fragrant waffles. Already on the table was homemade brown sugar syrup.

The children hardly had time to finish their breakfast before their governess, Miss Annie, appeared at the door. She was tall and thin with gentle eyes and sweet manners. Today she was wearing a dark grenadine, very simply made, but with the usual bustle.

"Come on, children," she said in her musical voice, without a hint of reproach. They followed her into the library.

When school and midday dinner were both over the children went to find their father in the study. He was sitting in an easy chair, and on the table beside him were great piles of books on agriculture. He was planning the farm work for the rest of the year. Right at his hand was a volume on grasses, for his greatest interest was to increase the beauties of the meadows and lawn, which already in a few short years he had developed from broomstraw and plantain into full emerald glory.

Birds were singing all around the house and the General interrupted his studies to explain their names and songs.

That reminded Lily. "Please come out and see the new nest I've found. I think it belongs to the blue grosbeaks."

The General agreed and soon all three left the vine-covered back porch and passed the numerous out-buildings which were part of a Virginia home. At Algoma they were mostly of the red stone quarried on the place. The prettiest of all was the dairy with its towers and turrets like a small feudal castle. It really had a three-fold purpose. One room had long pans of milk in frames, standing in cool water, and the next door was the entrance to Meta's studio. No one knew just what Meta studied but the place fascinated the children for it was outfitted entirely with rustic furniture, home-made from hickory, cedar, and split oak. It was always cool, as the ice cellar was underneath.

No Kennebec River wagon ran to Algoma, so it was necessary to save their own ice. The crop was harvested and hauled during the winter and put down between layers of straw, underneath the dairy, to be used during the summer.

Just behind the dairy they found the grosbeak's nest in a low bush. As they approached the flimsy structure, the shabby bluish-brown mother bird began to shudder with excitement. Her metallic "click-click" was repeated in quick and abusive succession; her tail spread like a redstart's and her crest rose high. But the handsome male, coated in lapis lazuli, sat discreetly on the fence at a safe distance, warbling continually. It seemed to the children that his notes stumbled over one another in their anxiety to be heard and admired. What a lovely, rippling song it was; not the wren's joyous bubbling as of a mountain fall— "Schnickelfritz, Schnickelfritz, Schnickelfritz"—but the contented serenity of a quiet stream.

In spite of the mother's fussiness, Lilybud and Lena peeped into the grassy nest and saw three furry fellows, with bills nearly as long as themselves. It was cruel to look further, for fear Madame Grosbeak might burst a blood vessel in her state of frenzy.

A moment later the grosbeak was scolding again, this time to a yellow-breasted chat.

Was the chat answering something saucy? It is a wonder how anything so small could make such an impudent racket and show such absolute cheek. After outscolding the grosbeak he proceeded to act for the children's benefit, ascending into the air, then tumbling clownishly down, chatting and caterwauling, saying a hundred different things in one breath, but never omitting that characteristic note of scolding.

Meanwhile Lilybud pushed her way impulsively into a blackberry thicket, not heeding the hissing snip of her dress, when it caught and tore on the clinging vines. She only rejoiced with the birds at all this good nesting material left so conveniently near their homes.

"Where are you taking us?" the others asked her breathlessly, as they clambered in her wake.

After fighting her way through some volunteer honeysuckle vines, she pushed back a low bush and pointed to what seemed a toy Dutch stove. "Did you ever see an oven bird keeping house?" she asked triumphantly.

The next was empty but the recent tenant was not far away. The little warbler, belying its reputation for shyness, looked at the child, quizzically, its head on one side. Then it walked slowly away, dignity in every line of its gold-crowned head and proudly arched breast, and with its tail held high.

"Listen! Oh, listen! The mate is beginning to sing. Did you ever hear an oven bird tuning up?" asked the General. "Can you hear how he starts off with his regular 'Teacher' note, so that you'll recognize it is his own air and not the indigo bunting's? Oh, look at him fly. As he warbles the rhythm of his song changes with his flight like the skylark's! If this little fellow doesn't want us to know who's singing, why does he begin with his regular 'Teacher' note, and if he does enjoy being heard why does he use his voice so seldom?"

"Doesn't he just tweedle-deedle-dee like any other bird?" asked Lena teasingly.

"But we must hurry to the house," exclaimed their father, not deigning to answer her question. "Are you so absorbed, fellows, that you don't see those dark clouds and feel the first scattering drops of rain on our poor heads?"

They hurried to the front piazza, and there watched the storm approach from many miles away. First they saw a curtain of rain like a mist across the azure Blue Ridge, then it came nearer on the Ragged Mountains, and on to the nearby hills. A moment later it had reached the river where they could not see it, but hear the soft fall of water on water. Then a sudden downpour drove the General and his daughters into the house.

Chapter XVII

Twilight
1890-1900

General Logan did not pass all of his country days in riding with his children and talking over farm projects with Mr. Stinson. Much of the time he spent walking up and down the library floor thinking out his new problems and planning telegrams and letters. How he would have loved the quick results of today's long distance calls!

There was a telephone at Algoma, but it was very primitive. You had to prepare your right forearm for a long siege of grinding the bell to evoke the special signals to reach any one of the ten or twelve subscribers of the strictly local line. To send a telegram you rang the railroad station with some sign such as three short rings and then a long one, while, let us say, Algoma's signal was three long and then a short ring; thus the calls were rung throughout the neighborhood. The wonderful thing was that your subconscious mind learned to respond only to your signal, unless you were so full of rural curiosity that you liked to take down almost any receiver to garner the news.

The General's telegrams gave little satisfaction to the curious, as those he sent to his secretary, Mr. Cox, in New York were usually in cipher. He had no regular amanuensis[16] at home, but dictated most of his wires and letters to Kate or the children. He was trading on the market a good deal at this time; also keeping up with his railroad interests and promotion work, both in the far South and the Northwest.

During this same year of 1890 he bought control of the Seattle, Lake Shore and Eastern Railroad which he soon sold at a large profit to the Northern Pacific. lxviii

The telautograph was his main occupation and he kept up with every smallest mechanical improvement in it. This interest called him to New York very frequently.

One day this spring the children had their usual feeling of dismay when their father appeared in the dark suit with a high stiff collar and large black cravat, which presaged a journey. This attire did not fit into his country personality. The worst of it this time was that Mother was leaving too. But they both promised to return before May 25 as that was their silver wedding anniversary.

This was to be a grand reunion as Jimmy and Meta would return from their schools and Katy and the Doctor were coming up from New Orleans, bringing with them their son, Thomas Muldrup Logan Bruns, born the August before.

---

[16] Scribe.-Ed.

Best of all, the children would have with them again their darling Mammy, who had been "lent" to Katy the winter before, to take care of the first grandchild. When the General heard his wife was sparing this Treasure he said, "Greater Love Than This Hath No Man!" He was right, although Lilybud-and-Lena felt the sacrifice was really theirs.

The weeks flew by and soon it was the day before the wedding anniversary. Only the family was at the silver wedding, but it numbered thirty. Many Logan cousins had by now arrived at Algoma. With his usual dignity, the General presided at one end of the long table. Kate, looking very lovely in a new dress of grey grosgrain with a real lace collar, did not take her usual place at the other end of the table but sat beside him. When opening her silver gifts she was as pleased as a child at a birthday party. So was Mully. It was a pity to break up such a happy house party, but the whole group had to hurry to Richmond a few days later for the unveiling of the Lee Monument on May 29th. It had been a long time since the General had made a Confederate oration, so he was glad to know that there would be many other speakers present and he need say only a few words of greeting.

Jim Conway drove the family up from 500 West Franklin to Monument Avenue. Kate realized with a pang that she must be getting old. This new Richmond above Monroe Park was changing rapidly and beginning to look "citified."

General Joseph E. Johnston unveiled the new monument to a crowd of thousands. The sight of so many acquaintances, including Wade Hampton and M.C. Butler, brought back sad memories for the

General and he welcomed the diverting hubbub of the cheering crowds.

The Washington Light Infantry Battalion presented Mrs. Logan with a commemorative gold-enameled pin. "Richmond, May 29th, 1890" was engraved on the streamer from which were suspended flags and shields of the Infantry and the Confederacy. On the back was engraved "W.L.I. to Mrs. General T.M. Logan".

It was hard for the General to break away next day and take the train for New York with his family. Soon after he escorted Mrs. Logan, Jimmie and Meta to the ship on which they were sailing for Europe.

After seeing his family off on their European journey, he returned to his deserted hotel suite. Here a sense of loneliness engulfed him. What would he do without them all, especially with no Kate around to look after him? With a rueful smile he remembered her parting words, "Now, General, don't get into any mischief while I'm away." Then he had an inspiration. He remembered the half serious discussions he had often had with his wife about doing over Algoma. She had objected to the disorder and confusion of carrying out any such plans. So he set about improving Algoma. He installed additional bathrooms, bought a new phonograph, built new walks, and so on. When his family returned from Europe, they were agreeably surprised, most of all Kate.

The future of his younger children, Meta and Lily, began to bother him. He wanted them to grow up better informed than the youngsters of his early days. His sister Lily had longed to go to college, but there was no such place for women in her day. Her namesake, little Lily, would attend college without question. Lilybud even talked of being a doctor, but the General didn't fancy that idea—doctoring was too far from dainty. Emerging from these thoughts came this main idea. The girls at the new Axtell Academy, an agricultural school, should have the same advantages as the boys. The Academy was completed in midsummer of 1892. It had two large rooms in front and one across the back. The General paid for the school and its equipment. The school board was at first not wholly enthusiastic, but in time, largely due to Meta's hard work on it, came around.

The school was a great success and at the end of the session Meta felt that her hard work had not been in vain. The following account is from the Algoma Log Book:

"The Axtell Academy held its first commencement exercises at six p.m., June 3rd, 1893. There was an assemblage of one hundred people, who listened with great interest to Mr. Charles Edward Bolling's speech. Then Miss Margaret P. Logan delivered the three medals for scholarship, attendance and improvement. Miss Lillian Stinson received the scholarship medal, Miss Nowell the one for attendance, and Walker Gilmer the one for improvement.

"Miss Emma Barksdale of Richmond then responded to the demand for music by playing on the banjo accompanied by the glee club from Algoma. The children were charmed by the music and encored tremendously. The scholars were served with cake, candy and lemonade, which pleased them perhaps even more than the prizes."

In June, 1892, when the Commencement exercises were held at the University of Virginia, near Charlottesville, about thirty miles from Algoma, the Logans attended, as Jimmie was to receive his diploma in history and his cousin Edwin P. Cox was to graduate in law.

After the ceremonies the General, Mrs. Logan and their guest visited the University of Virginia, founded and built by Thomas Jefferson, author of the Declaration of Independence. Wandering under the shady arcades, peering down half hidden vistas with their glimpses of boxwood, shade trees and rose in fragrant bloom, they finally stopped to inspect the peculiar serpentine walls. This winding effect was a clever idea of Jefferson's. He wanted to economize, and yet make the work strong and lasting, as indeed it proved, for the walls were still in perfect condition after almost a century.

Nearby the General pointed out the home of the author of the McGuffey readers. He had been a much loved Professor at the University and in spite of being a Yankee had weathered the storms of war in the sixties, remaining at this Southern University throughout the conflict. He had lived in one of the houses at the end of the sweeping lawn which starts in front of the University Rotunda, built by Jefferson.

Life at Algoma was almost a continuous round of gaiety. Sunday morning, of course, was devoted to church—if accessible, or services were often held in the parlor. On Sunday afternoons a large cavalcade always went walking. A gun was carried strictly for protection, as Mrs. Logan did not approve of hunting on Sunday even when a hunting houseparty was in progress. Such was the gusto which marked all activities at Algoma that even the singing of hymns, also specified on Sundays in preference to less reverent ditties, was enthusiastic and often continued until midnight.

To celebrate a birthday, secret trips were made to bazaars at Jonesboro and Howardsville. All kinds of foolish gadgets and tokens were also concocted at home to tease or please the recipient. Original poems and verses were written to order for birthday or wedding anniversaries. Dainties and cakes were likewise made by the most expert cake bakers in the household.

When there was no birthday to celebrate, after supper whist was in order. There were no stakes but a continuous tournament. Other members of the household read aloud, wrote letters, or played games such as consequences, conundrums or twenty questions. These were often varied by more artistic questions. These were often varied by more artistic performances like Magic Music and Poetical Dominoes. The General was especially fond of watching others act out charades. Mrs. Logan was resourceful, both in choosing words and in finding original costumes for these plays.

Every evening ended in singing. Two favorites at this time were "When Love in Kind," and "I'll Never Forget My Dolly."

The visitors at Algoma called themselves Algomaniacs. This group had a hunting party in late October, 1892. Those present were Irene Langhorne, the original "Gibson Girl," Berta and Sallie Wellford, Elizabeth Strother, Emily Nolting, Nannie Lay and Mary Cox. The men were Blair Bolling, James L. Anderson, F.D. Williams, Frederic Scott, George

Gibson, John Franklin Alexander, Legh R. Page and the author, Thomas Nelson Page.

In the log book for October 22nd, 1892, we find: "Meta and Mary got up at six-thirty and gave the hunters breakfast. Then they went to the depot to meet Miss Irene Langhorne and Mr. Legh Page of Richmond. In the afternoon, Miss Berta Wellford, Miss Mary Cox and Messrs. Bolling and Page drove to Mr. Alexander's. Later Miss Langhorne and Mr. Page went horseback riding and the rest went hunting again. After dinner Miss Langhorne sang and played for everybody to dance. There was a reading by Mr. Page."

Mr. Thomas Nelson Page's reading was from Marse Chan and his personality and charming voice had everyone near to tears. Lilybud was weeping outright. As soon as she had dried her eyes, she went up to Mr. Page. "How do you find time to write?" she asked shyly. "I'd like to be an author too, but I've been too busy to do anything like that for several years."

Mr. Page smiled sympathetically—not a bit teasingly, as Lily had feared he might. "Can you let me see your work?" he asked, really interested.

Lily ran upstairs and came back holding out a mottled, rather grimy notebook. She opened it and show[ed] the scratchy pages, then looked up in delighted surprise. "You didn't say it," she exclaimed.

"Say what, my dear child?"

"That I must be a chicken myself, the way I write! Grown people think it's clever to say that."

"Well, I don't. But I think this book is clever. I love the way you have each chicken on a separate page, with a full history and character study of each one.

Now, this rooster, for instance, that mothered the baby chicks! And Gray-Around-The-Neck—the best fighter on the yard! Why, my dear, if this book were mine I could make a fortune from it!"

The others laughed, but Lilybud was much encouraged. She knew Mr. Page liked the whole family and she hoped she would have his help and inspiration many times throughout the years. But this was not to be. Mr. Page liked all the Logans, but there was one main attraction for him at Algoma. He was then a widower in his forties and his great grief at losing his first wife had not tended to make him look any younger than his years. In spite of this, he had set his heart on the General's seventeen-year-old daughter, Meta. She liked him, too, but it would have taken quite a while and much patience to bridge the years and temperaments between the two. Mr. Page was in no waiting mood. In the spring of 1893, he came one day to the Logan's Richmond house at 500 West Franklin and presented his ultimatum.

"I'm going to Florida," he said. "Please give me a positive answer now. If you won't have me, someone else will."

Meta had heard threats like that before. She did not take this one very seriously. She only laughed and talked about what the two of them would do the next summer at Algoma. She was quite shocked to hear soon afterwards that Mr. Page had made good his threat and had married somebody else in Florida.

Thus Algoma suffered the loss of one of its most delightful guests. But to return to that autumn of 1892, when Mr. Page was still a member of the Algoma circle. Like all other good things these happy house parties could not go on forever. The 1903 panic was already on the way and General Logan had to stick close to New York. This depression was more trying for him than the earlier one in the seventies, for then he was accustomed to privation. But he came through somehow.

Just as matters seemed to be working out favorably there was the threat of Bryan and free silver, which General Logan considered a fallacy. He was so much interested in the subject that he consented to take the Chairmanship of the Virginia Gold Democratic Party in 1896. He was too busy to electioneer in the country, leaving that to Mrs. Logan who "stumped" in his favor.

General Logan kept up his principle of giving out as much work as possible at Algoma, the home which a little colored boy had once called "Heaven". This place was, so tradition says, a former hunting ground of the father of Pocahontas, the Indian chief Powhatan. He is supposed to have located a deep hole in the river and called the nearby country "Algoma", meaning "Deep Water". The best fish with which the General stocked his ponds had come from this down-reaching basin near the low-grounds.

Chapter XVIII

A Parade of the
Years—Twentieth Century

G reat changes came with the turn of the century. The house in Richmond was sold and family life centered now at Algoma. The farm did not seem remote and cut off any more for the General had been largely instrumental in the installation of a bridge at Howardsville. This took the place of the picturesque but most inconvenient ferry.

About halfway between the bridge and Algoma was the new Bruns home, Dungannon, built on land the General had given his eldest daughter. With the aid and advice of her husband and father Katy had cleverly utilized the native brown stone to make for herself and family a French chateau with towers and turrets. Ivy was already being coaxed to creep up the rough outside walls. Inside the house Dr. and Mrs. Bruns had shown much foresight in completely paneling the walls—using pine upstairs and oak on the lower floor. This obviated all the disorder and expense of repainting and papering. Dungannon had plenty of room for the rapidly growing family. Little Logan Bruns now had three brothers—John Dickson, James Henry and Thomas Nelson Carter.

Early in 1896 Meta had married Hartwell Cabell of Cincinnati and Edgewood, Virginia. Their son Philip Francis was born late that year, and their daughter Honoria Muldrup in 1902.

Before leaving Algoma, Meta had arranged for the county to take over the library and schoolhouse with rights for full use of the buildings and all equipment, as long as the place was needed. The General was sure he could not run the Academy without Meta. They both now felt their work had been worthwhile, for several of the scholars already were well started toward success.

By this time the General had relinquished his railroad interests. His last big deal was in the early nineties, when he bought control of the Seattle, Lake Shore and Eastern Railroad, selling it later at a good profit to the Northern Pacific.[lxix] Now he was concentrating all his energies on the development of the telautograph.

In 1900 Foster Ritchie constructed a variable current telautograph machine. This immediately caused all instruments of the motor operating friction drive, escapement type to become obsolete and work on them was abandoned.

Mr. G.S. Tiffany, the experimental engineer of the Company, soon after developed a special variable current instrument which in 1901 he covered by patents. These still form the basis of the patent protection of the American telautograph.[lxx] This newer machine proved a great attraction at the patent office of the Pan-American exhibition that year.

About this time the children overheard a discussion between the General and Mr. Gray, the inventor of the telautograph, about the possibilities of a future air-ship. "A charming, picturesque idea but impracticable," they both concluded.

In 1901 and early 1902 trials were made at Fort Wadsworth, New York, to test the reliability of the telautograph service between range-finding stations and the emplacement pits of guns in coast fortifications. The success of these trials resulted in a large order from the government. Telautographs were then placed in the eight coast Forts in the New London and Newport districts. This installation was completed in time for joint army and navy maneuvers in August, 1902. The operation of the instruments during gun fire was so satisfactory that subsequent orders were placed (in 1903) for complete equipment of Fort Barrancas and Fort Pickens, at Pensacola, Florida, and also for the forts of Portland, Maine. In the meantime commercial development of the machine had been going ahead. The first bank installation was made in 1903 at the old Mercantile National Bank, Broadway and Dey Street, New York, where the machine was used for communication between paying teller and bookkeeper. Other banks followed suit. Then came the adoption of telautographs by several wholesale companies in 1903.

Working with General Logan on the telautograph was his son, James Henry (Jimmie) who in April, 1903, married Elizabeth Hagerman in New York.

Lena was married the same June, at Algoma, to Douglas Forsyth of New Orleans. General and Mrs. Logan felt as if losing their "baby" was the saddest of all changes, but much of the sting was moved when the young couple promised to spend their summers in Virginia. Lily this time did not hide behind the sofa and write tear-streaked poems of farewell, but her grief was even more poignant that it had been at Katy's wedding, Lilybud and Lena had always been inseparable.

To dispel her loneliness Lily immersed herself more and more in her books. In 1897 she had graduated at Newcomb College in New Orleans; in1900 she had taken her A.M. degree at Columbia University in New York, specializing in chemistry. The General cooperated with her every step of the way. It was as if he were going to college all over again with his daughter. Great was his shock therefore when in the midst of a course leading here to a PhD., she announced her intention to marry a Cincinnati attorney, Albert H. Morrill, a McGuffey descendant. Theirs was an outdoor wedding, just two years after Lena's. Lily comforted her parents with the promise to return soon and often to Algoma. The young couple then went off on a camping trip into the mountains.

During the summer of 1905 the motor car came to Buckingham County. Mr. William Henderson of New Orleans had bought one of the risky affairs and had it sent to Algoma while he travelled more safely on the train.

After the car was duly set up and the motor started with a spitting pother, the whole of Algoma household, including the darkies, came to the front of the house to discover what made all that racket. They were astounded to see Mr. Henderson's red automobile. This was a roomy affair, with lots of space, not only to stay in but also to fall out of. The front seat was especially precarious as everything was open and defenseless. A tumble would mean going down some distance, for the car seats were up so high that one felt as if one were on top of a tallyho. However, it did not look as if one would fall out yet, because in spite of all the preparatory noises the monster refused to go forward even for the first small exhibition trip around the Algoma circle.

"Won't you come driving with me, General, and bring Lilybud and Lena along too?" asked Mr. Henderson.

Although they accepted, they seemed to have some misgivings; but after drinking in the fearsome beauty of this new kind of transportation, Lilybud and Lena went leisurely upstairs and enveloped themselves in grey train dusters. These had belonged to dear old Aunt Nernie, who had died some years before. In preparation for the drive the two young people had already put long ribbon strings to their hats and tied these under their chins. As if this were not enough protection, they had reinforced the streamers with enveloping veils to hold down their large hats. It shortly proved that veils and streamers alike were really needed.

With a great deal of cranking, plus pushing and shoving by the darkies, the creature of tin and wood was at last on its way. Everything went along quite smoothly on the farm road where the adventurers met no one, but after they came out on the pike near the school house the situation altered. Horses, which for years had been humbled into semi-immobility by age and privation, became galvanized into life at sight of red Behemoth. Many near accidents resulted. Finally Mr. Henderson decided to come to a halt when he saw a horse even in the bluest distance. This necessitated continual stopping and starting and the trouble was that when the car once halted it didn't seem to want to start again. With all these delays the five-mile circuit took just one hour. On their return to Algoma Lilybud and Lena felt very travelled in comparison to the stay-at-homes who had been afraid to take the trip. The General was more than ever convinced that he was right in not having invested time and money in the motor car industry.

By this time there were quite a number of grandchildren. The General loved to call this new generation anything but their right names. One of them retaliated by giving him the name of "Go-Go." This probably derived from General Logan because he was called "The General" by everybody in the place. He seldom spoke of his wife as Kate but always as "Your Mother," or "Your Grandmother," as the case might be.

One of his grandchildren, John Dickson Bruns, later wrote this account of himself and "Go-Go":

And I remember reading late one night,

Shelley and Keats and Browning, I suppose,

When he came in with sparkle in his eye

Smiling at me and looking down his nose.

"What, funny fellow," he then chuckling said,

"Reading again from the heroic dead?

The more you learn the lesser still you know

I'll quote the sage who said so long ago:

'I, too, when young did eagerly frequent

Doctor and Saint, and heard great argument

About it and about, but evermore

Come out at the same door wherein I went!'"

"Learning for learning's sake, unapplied to human needs, is only dust and ashes," was the General's idea. But he knew that applied knowledge could be valuable and for that reason he had always encouraged Lily in her college ambitions.

For college in the nineties was still unusual for girls. A friend once said to Kate: "Mrs. Logan, your daughter will never get a husband if you let her persist in going to college!"

The speaker's daughter intervened: "But Mamma, how do you know such things? You never went to college—you never so much as read a book."

"Yes, I did too!" she turned indignantly to another daughter. "Susie, what was the name of that green-backed book I read?"

All this time in spite of numerous discouragements, General Logan contrived to concentrate his energies on the telautograph, holding on to the idea that this machine would one day rival the telephone.

Mrs. Logan, who had more than her share of woman's intuition, begged him over and over again to go back to his old way of spreading his interests in several directions.

At Algoma one late autumn day Kate stood near a study window watching brown leaves steadily falling. A feeling of winter was in the air. Kate saw it, smelt it, heard it, as the wind moaned around the windows. Leaving the window she went over to the leather couch where the General was lying half asleep. She drew over him a Roman blanket—a souvenir of one of her trips abroad. She felt the room was not warm enough in spite of the brightly glowing log fire. The rusty chrysanthemums on the table drooped as if already frost-bitten before being picked.

The General's old war wounds were troubling him more and more these days. It made Kate very sad to see him lie there instead of walking up and down the room with his hands behind his back—the way he used to do when pondering problems—and there had always been problems to ponder!

She seated herself in the General's worn leather chair—which she had never felt willing to replace—so much was it bound up with their early life. These days were like autumn with dying leaves and acrid fading chrysanthemums. Once they had been young—full of energy and happy ambition. How many of those earlier ambitions had been fulfilled? she wondered.

Her General had certainly done his part in awakening the South to its new position and duties. In the very hotbeds of Confederate Sectionalism he had sounded the first notes of Reconciliation and Nationalization. He had also given a clarion call for education of the once disfranchised. He had done his part in arousing Richmond and the South generally to the importance of railroad development.

In his private life he had given help and refuge to numerous members of his family and hers, both in Richmond and in the country. The plantation life at Algoma had set an example of culture and hospitality, improving the outlook of the many who had visited there. He had given help and work to the needy and had built up the country side. What more could one man hope for and expect?

"What a pity I have to go back to New York," her husband's voice awakened her from her revery.

"Oh, General, why do you go?" she entreated. "You are no longer able to push something new and untried. Why don't you retire from the telautograph company, give up your New York apartment and stay here all the time? You can bring your secretary with you and take up your writing and your railroad interests."

The General rose to a sitting position and opened his eyes wide in amazement. "Am I the kind to leave anything I've put my hand to?" he asked. "Besides, the business is going on splendidly now."

He was right this time. By 1914 there was still more reason for encouragement. The machine had become practical and its use was growing rapidly. In spite of General Logan's own failing health his hopes were high, for optimism had always been his leading characteristic. In a spirit of optimism he had entered the War, putting aside the studies which had heretofore absorbed most of his attention, leaving the family and friends who had absorbed all his affection.

This quality had made him take desperate risks as a skirmish officer and had carried him safely and cheerfully through privation, bodily injury and defeat. To him, defeat meant an opportunity to being again—not so much for himself but for the South and the whole nation of which he was a part.

In 1867 he was already pleading for relief for the poverty stricken citizens of Manchester, Virginia.[lxxi] A few years later he began to write leaders concerning the railroad interest of Richmond.[lxxii] He had already decided that the development of railroads would help most in building up the South. In spite of his own hard work for his growing family, from then on he continued his writing, advocating every kind of betterment for his town and the South.[lxxiii]

He conquered his own shyness in order to give lectures on constructive subjects such as schools, development of the South, and urging nationalization.[lxxiv] Finally he returned to his earlier interest—a building up of the South through the expansion of its railroad systems. Here his optimism came most to the fore, when he turned defeat into victory in 1886.[lxxv] Now defeat was near again in the worst of all possible phases—illness and death. But even his optimism rose to the surface and he refused to admit the advance of the enemy.

Then came the World War! Knowing what war meant, the General realized that all lesser interests would be submerged in the one absorbing task of fighting. He felt that the telautograph would be kept at a standstill when there was no time to lose, for his own health was growing worse. Years ago he had given all the force of his youth to fighting for his own section of the country, and the wounds from that war were still taking their toll. He had always loved life, but there was no strength left to face this new conflict. Bright's disease and tuberculosis of the lower spine soon conquered him.

He died on Tuesday, August 11th, 1914, at his New York apartment. Two days later there was a sad meeting in Richmond when the General's family and old friends of the happy Algoma days gathered together to do him honor. He was laid to rest in Richmond's beautiful Hollywood Cemetery, where are also buried Generals J.E.B. Stuart, Fitzhugh Lee, George Edward Pickett, and Confederate President Jefferson Davis. Mrs. Logan, who died of apoplexy on February 10, 1915, was buried beside him in the same cemetery.

The End

Bibliography

(Unpublished)

A record of the Logan family, by George William Logan and Lily Logan Morrill, Cincinnati, Ohio, 1923.

A Miniature Epic, by Samuel Logan, Picayune Print, New Orleans, 1887.

A War Correspondence, saved by my mother, Mrs. Sophronia Lucia Hutson, (nee Palmer) 1861—lent by C.W. Hutson.

Booklet of Washington Light Infantry, Charleston, South Carolina, February, 1873.

Pamphlet, Reception of General T.M. Logan by the Washington Light Infantry, July, 1875.

Framed Resolutions of the Washington Light Infantry Battalion concerning the unveiling of the Lee Monument, May 29th, 1890 in Richmond, printed by E. Perry & Co.

Framed resolutions, in script, of Washington Light Infantry at the Armory, in Charleston, S.C., June 5th, 1890, concerning the Richmond meeting.

War Department: Publication Office, War Records 1861-65, Washington, May 16th, 1881.

Bibliographical data on Colonel George William Logan, Jr., by his son, Edmund du Fossat Logan.

Letters to and from Colonel George William Logan, 1863-64, saved by his family in New Orleans.

Letter and card from General Beauregard to General Logan; in possession of the author, Lily Logan Morrill.

Letter of northern soldier picked up on the battlefield, near Camp Fair Oaks, June 26th, 1862. In possession of the author.

An Interview of Major William A. Watts, by W.W. Ball, editor of the The News and Courier, Charleston, S.C., November 27th, 1932, with letter written to Mrs. H.D. Bruns.

Letters of Judge Edwin P. Cox to Lily Logan Morrill, March 13th, 1934,—April 21st, 1934.

Numerous letter concerning General Logan's promotions. Copies of these are in possession of the author. (My Confederate Girlhood, page 66)

Letter to Colonel Logan from Colonel A.C. Haskell. Subject: Relative ranks of the two colonels, Columbia, S.C., July 21st, 1864.

Letter of congratulation to General Logan on his promotion. Signed: Stephanus Ford, March 8th, 1865.

Letter about scarcity of forage (given in text). Sent to General Logan by George W. Melton, Major General, Nelson, N.C., April 7th, 1865.

Letter to General Logan from his sister Lily, describing Sherman's raid on Columbia, S.C., March 2nd, 1865.

Letter to General T.M. Logan from Lily Logan, written in Columbia, S.C., September 3rd, 1865.

Letter to General Logan from his father, George W. Logan, Sr., written in Columbia, S.C., February 12th, 1866.

Letter from Kate Virginia Cox (Logan) to her brother Edwin, May 7th, 1861, Clover Hill, Va.

For My Children—Some Days of Mother's Life, by Georgie Logan de Saussure, written in 1921.

Lee: The Final Achievement, 1865-1870, by Frances Pendleton Gaines, an address delivered before the Southern Society of New York.

Handwritten war account of General Logan by a comrade in arms from Headquarters, Second Brigade, S.C. Division, U.C.V. Aiken, S.C.

Autobiography of William P. deSaussure, pamphlet, printed 1929.

Letter from S.S. Boyee, of the Indianapolis Chamber of Commerce, May 13th, 1876.

Letter from Post-master General D.M. Key, July 8th, 1877, to General Logan, written in Boston, January 23rd, 1877.

Letter from Wade Hampton to T.M. Logan, February 7th, 1873.

Notes (in script) by Katie Logan Bruns, on Richmond life of the eighties.

Letter from Lulu Logan Bentley to Lena L. Forsyth.

Letter to Lily Logan Morrill by C.E.A. McCarthy, Secretary of the Southern Railway Co., March 14th, 1934.

Letter to Lily Logan Morrill, from Richard J. Johnston, librarian, Bureau of Railway Economics, Washington, D.C., March 13th, 1933.

History of the Telautograph, from printed pamphlet of the company. Letter to Lily Logan Morrill from C.H. George, President, February 23rd, 1934. Letter to Mrs. Logan from General Logan's friend and associate in the Telautograph, Mr. John Franklin Alexander, who thus describes the

General: "The nerve that never relaxes, the eye that never wanders, the thought that never falters—these are the masters of victory." January 1887.

The Algoma Log Book.

Bibliography

(Published)

Delta of May 18th, 1851, as quoted in New Orleans Time-Picayune, May 18th, 1914.

L.H. Bailey, Cyclopedia of Horticulture, page 1510.

For further research on the history of the Logan family and of early Charleston, consult the following: A Day on Cooper River, by John B. Irving and Louisa Stoney, second edition, R.L. Bryan Co., Columbia, S.C., 1932. Grose's Antiquities of Scotland; Forsyth's Beauties and Legends of Scotland; Robertson's History of Scotland; Buchannon's History of Scotland; Mclan's Costumes of the Clans with Letter Pieces by James Logan, David Bryce & Co., Glasgow; James Sixth and the Gowrie Mystery, by Andrew Lang. Ramsey's History of South Carolina; River Sketches of South Carolina Colonial History, and Carroll's Historical Collections of South Carolina. The Charleston Public Library has a valuable collection of Charlestoniana, including the small part remaining of Martha Daniell Logan's Gardener's Kalendar. These sources are given in A Record of the Logan Family, by

George William Logan and Lily Logan Morrill. Unfortunately, many of these books are now rare. See also, Logan Family Records, vol. VII, May 1917, no. 5, Whole NO. 97.

Genealogy, A Monthly Magazine of American Ancestry, William M. Clemens, publisher, Hackensack, N.J.

My Confederate Girlhood, by Kate Virginia Logan and Lily Logan Morrill, Garrett & Massie, publishers, Richmond, Virginia.

The Military Operations of General Beauregard, by Alfred Roman, Harper & Brothers, New York, 1883.

The Women of the Confederacy, by Francis B. Simpkins and James Patton, Garrett & Massie, publishers, Richmond, Va., 1936.

Charleston, S.C. News and Courier, July 22nd, 1891, The Memory of Manassas, unveiling of Washington Light Infantry obelisk.

Time-Dispatch, Richmond, Va., July 27th, 1936. Letter from Robert M. Wallace about Designer of Stars and Bars.

See also Confederate Scrap Book, J.L. Hill Printing Co., for the benefit of the Memorial Bazaar, Richmond, Va. 1893, page 126.

The Epic of America, by James Truslow Adams, Little Brown & Co., Boston.

Richmond, Virginia, Times Dispatch for August 12th, 1914. Notice of General Logan's death with biographical data.

Club Life, New York, 1897. Biography of General Logan.

Edgefield, S.C. Advertiser, January 30th, 1878, Notes on Logan's Career.

A Diary with Reminiscences of the War and Refugee Life in the Shenandoah Valley, 1860-65, by Mrs. Cornelia McDonald, Cullom & Ghertner Co., Nashville, Tenn., 1934.

The Story of the Confederacy, by Robert Self Henry, the Bobbs-Merrill Co., Indianapolis, 1931.

Men of Mark in Virginia, by Lyon G. Tyler, Men of Mark Publishing Co., Washington, D. C., 1908.

Wearing of the Grey, by John Esten Cooke, E B. Treat & Co., New York, 1867.

Recollections and Letters of Robert E. Lee, by his son, Captain Robert E. Lee, Garden City Publishing Co., Inc., Garden City, New York (reprint) 1924.

R.E. Lee, A Biography, by Douglas Freeman, Charles Scribner's Sons, N.Y., 1935. (Vol. 4, pp. 60 and 61, General Lee's dinner at Clover Hill.)

Memoirs of Robert E. Lee, by A.L. Long, B.F. Johnson & Co., Richmond, Va., 1886.

Lee of Virginia, by William E. Brooks, Garden City Publishing Co., Garden City, N.Y., 1932.

A Constitutional View of the Late War between the States, vol. I, by Alexander H. Stephens, National Publishing Co. Philadelphia, Pa., 1868.

The War of the Rebellion, a compilation of the Official Records of the Union and Confederate Armies, Series I, vol. I, Government Printing Office, Washington, 1880.

Butler and His Cavalry, by W.R. Brooks, the State Company, Columbia, S.C., 1909.

Reminiscences of Peace and War, by Mrs. Roger A. Pryor, Grosset & Dunlap, New York, 1908.

The Genesis of the Civil War, Samuel W. Crawford, N.Y., 1887.

Age of Hate, George Fort Milton, Coward McCann, 1930. Eve of Conflict, same author, Houghton Mifflin & Co., Boston, 1934.

Virginia's Attitude Toward Slavery and Secession, by Beverly B. Munford, Longmans Green & Co., New York, 1909.

Recollections of a Confederate Staff Officer, by General G. Moxley Sorrell, the Neale Publishing Co., New York and Washington, 1905.

Military Memoirs of a Confederate, by E.P. Alexander, Charles Scribner's Sons, 1907, p. 470.

The Rise and Fall of the Confederate Government, by Jefferson Davis, D. Appleton & Co., New York, 1881.

Advance and Retreat, by J.B. Hood. Published for the Hood Orphan Memorial Fund, G.T. Beauregard, New Orleans, La., 1880.

The Photographic History of the Civil War, the Review of Reviews Co., N.Y., 1911.

Last Headquarters, by Bill Sharpe, Richmond Times-Dispatch, Sunday Magazine section, November 20th, 1938.

The V.M.I. New Market Cadets, by William Couper, the Michie Co., Charlottesville, Va., 1933.

Acts of the General Assembly of the State of Virginia, 1859-60, William F. Ritchie, Public Printer, Richmond, Va., 1860.

Who's the Patriot? By Mrs. Flora McDonald Williams, Courier Journal Job Printing Co., Louisville, Ky., 1886.

Is Davis a Traitor? By Alfred Taylor Bledsoe, the Hermitage Press, Inc., Richmond, Va., 1907.

The Virginia Plutarch, vol. II, by Philip Alexander Bruce, the University of North Carolina Press, Chapel Hill, N. C., 1929.

Morrill

Battles and Leaders of the Civil War, Century Co., 1884-8, vol. 3 p. 746, Knoxville; vol. 4, pp 200 and 208, Drewry's Bluff.

Richmond Dispatch, Dec. 31st, 1867, Welfare Meeting.

From Dixie: Original articles by Southern Writers, published as a souvenir of the Memorial Bazaar, West, Johnson & Co., Richmond, Va., 1893.

The Tragic Era, by Claude G. Bowers, Houghton, Mifflin & Co., Boston, 1929.

"Palmetto," writing from Charleston, S.C. to Richmond Dispatch, for July 28th, 1875, concerning reunion of Hampton Legion, Columbia, S.C., July 21st, 1875. Also concerning General Logan's talk at that time on industrial future of the South and his tributes to Jackson and Lee.

Harper's Weekly, August 14th, 1875.

N.Y. Daily Tribune, October 11th, 1875. Richmond, Va. Whig, "Personal", July 27th, 1875.

Petersburg, Va., Index and Appeal, July 28th, 1875.

Richmond Daily Enquirer, July 24th, 1875.

Richmond (Va.) Dispatch, December 31st, 1877, as quoted in Richmond Virginia Times Dispatch, December 31st, 1917.

Richmond Times Dispatch, July 12th, 1932, Dr. Thomas H. Reed: "Our Presidents today may be mothered in New York, but our best political ideas are fathered in Virginia."

General Logan's speech before Hood's Texas Brigade, as published in the Evening Edition of Waco (Texas) Examiner, June 27th, 1877. Referred to and quoted from, in part, in Galveston News, June 28th, 1877; N.Y. Herald, June 28th, 1877; Petersburg Index Appeal; and The Houston Age.

General T.M. Logan's Tribute to Lee, News Leader, Richmond, Va., January 19th, 1909.

Sunday Mercury, January 16th, 1887 (R.R.'s).

The Education of the People, by James Augustus St. John; Chapman & Hall, London, 1858.

Dictionary of American Biography, Charles Scribner's Sons, New York. (General Logan's Biography).

Richmond (Va.) News Leader, February 11th, 1939. (Justice). On Logan's connection with railroads.

Charleston (S.C.) Sunday News, December 12th, 1886. (R.R.'s).

Washington Critic, November 20-30, 1886. (R.R.'s).

Financial Record, November 20th,1886. (R.R.'s).

The State, Richmond, Va., November 20th, 22nd, 24th, 26th, and December 6th, 7th, and 17th, 1886. (R.R.'s).

Morrill

The Daily Graphic, N.Y. Wall Street, November 22nd, 1886. (R.R.'s).

New York Herald, November 21st, 1886. (R.R.'s).

New York Sun, November 21st, 1886. (R.R.'s).

Atlanta Constitution, November 20th and 26th, 1886. (R.R.'s).

Cincinnati Enquirer, November 30th, 1886.

Town Topics, November 18th, 1886. (R.R.'s).

The Daily Stockholder, November 26th 1886, (R.R.'s).

The Hour, November 27th, 1886. (R.R.'s).

For further research on the railroads, the following may be consulted: Report on the Internal Commerce of the United States, by U.S. Bureau of Statistics (Treasury Dept.) for 1886; Washington, Government Printing Office, 1886, States of Virginia, North Carolina, South Carolina, Georgia, Florida, etc. Fairfax Harrison's History of the Legal Development of the Railroad System of the Southern Railway Company, Washington, D.C., 1901. See also American Railroad Journal and Railway World from 1870 to 1887. For change of gauge see the following: Railway World, March 27th, 1875, pp 20-25, and January 2nd, 1875; The Change of Gauge of Southern Railroads, in 1886, C. H. Hudson, printed in the Railroad Gazette, October 14th, 1887, p. 668; November 11, 1887, pp 731-733, and in Scientific American Supplement, December 3rd and 10th, 1887, pp 9935-9937 and 9946-9947.

The South, December 11th, 1886. (R.R.'s).

The Investigator, November 30th, 1886. (R.R.'s).

Raleigh Christian Advocate (N.C.), December 1st, 1886. (R.R.'s).

Oscar Willoughby Riggs' article on General Logan's R.R. work, Richmond, Va. Dispatch, April 9th, 1887.

New York Daily Tribune, May 3rd, 1887. (R.R.'s).

Sketch of Samuel Fulton Covington's life by J.E. Bradford, Miami (Ohio) University Bulletin, October 1914.

Richmond (Va.) State, May 12th, 1877; Enquirer, May 14th, 1877. (R.R.'s). Richmond Dispatch, November 20th, 21st and 23rd and 30th, 1886; December 9th, 1886; April 10th, 1887.

New York Mail and Express, November 20th and 27th, 1886. (R.R.'s).

Richmond Times Dispatch (Va.) August 12th, 1914. (R.R.'s). Lexington Gazette and Citizen (Va.) March 23rd, 1882. (R.R.'s).

Richmond News Leader, (Va.) August 12th, 1914. (R.R.'s).

Richmond, Virginia in Old Prints, 1737-1887, Alexander Wilbourne Weddell, Johnson Publishing Co., 1932.

Richmond Homes and Memories, by Robert Beverly Munford, Jr., Garrett & Massie, publishers, Richmond, Va.

St. Paul's Church, Richmond, Va.; Its Historic Years and Memorials, Elizabeth Wright Weddell, William Byrd Press, Inc., Richmond, Va.

Sunday Magazine Section, Richmond Times Dispatch, Sunday, November 11th, 1932. Immigrant Boy to St. Paul's Rector, by Vera Palmer.

The same, December 16th, 1934: First German Calls Virginia's Four Hundred.

The same, October 4th, 1936: Progress Downs Another Richmond Shrine, (Old Valentine Studio), by Vera Palmer.

The same, November 22nd, 1936: Ha'ants Don't Worry Centenarians of Clover Hill, by Rose Trueheart. (Includes quotation about General Lee's dinner at Clover Hill from My Confederate Girlhood, pp 70-71.

The History of Chesterfield County, Virginia, by Edwin P. Cox, Chesterfield Court House, September 11th, 1936.

ADDITIONAL HISTORY OF WAR RECORDS, CYCLOPEDIA, NEWSPAPER AND OTHER SKETCHES OF LIFE OF GENERAL T.M. LOGAN: FROM SOME OF WHICH EXTRACTS HAVE BEEN SELECTED FOR THIS RECORD.

January 6th, 1865. To M.C. Butler, recommending Colonel Logan for promotion, "As I regard him as one of the very best officers of his rank in the service."

Wade Hampton, Major General.

January 6th, 1865. To General S. Cooper, recommending promotion of Colonel Logan to the rank of Brigadier General. "I refer the Department with confidence to the opinions of General Robert E. Lee, Lt. General Longstreet, Lt. General Ewell, Major General Hampton and Brigadier General Gary, as to his qualifications for command."

M.C. Butler, Major General.

And numerous similar letters of promotion, etc. in possession of the author. (See My Confederate Girlhood, p. 66)

Form filled out by James H. Logan for South Carolina College Alumni, July 12th, 1906.

Article from Who's Who in America, edition 1906-7, vol. 4, p. 1094.

Morrill

Article from Herringshaw's American Biography.

Article from National Cyclopedia of American Biography, published by James T. White & Co., New York, 1900, vol. 1, p. 472.

Article from America's Successful Men, edited by Henry Hall and published by the New York Tribune, vol. 2, pp. 506-9.

Article by Marion J. Verdery from News and Courier, Charleston, S.C., May 10th, 1899.

Certificate of Association of Army of Northern Virginia, Virginia Division—dated September 27th, 1876.

Commission as Brigadier General signed by John C. Breckenridge, Secretary of War, dated February 23rd, 1865.

Transfer Order signed by General W. H. Taylor, dated February 28th, 1865.

Statement from Major General Butler to General Cooper, dated December 31st, 1864, as to rank of Colonel Aikens and Rutledge, with endorsement thereon by General R.E. Lee, under date of March 15th, 1862.

Biographical Catalogue of the Portraits in the Confederate Memorial Institute, The Battle Abbey.

Random Recollections, by Beverly B. Munford, pp 235-237, printed 1905.

Virginia Historical Magazine, vol. 23, no. 2, April 1915, page 24.

The Algoma Log Book

Necrology

Richmond (Va.) Times Dispatch, August 12th, 1914.

Cincinnati Enquirer, August 13th, 1914.

Mobile (Ala.) Item, August 12th, 1914.

Albany Evening Journal, August 12th, 1914.

New York Evening Journal, August 12th, 1914.

Holyoke (Mass.) Transcript, August 12th, 1914.

Hartford (Conn.) Times, August 12th, 1914.

New York Herald, August 13th, 1914.

Providence, (R.I.) August 12th, 1914.

Richmond (Va.), August 12th, 1914.

Minneapolis Journal, August 12th, 1914.

Town & Country, New York, August 22nd, 1914.

List of General Logan's Own Writings, Cultural and Social

Jefferson and Hamilton (in script), June 9th, 1878.

Education and Progress (pamphlet), address delivered before the Educational Association of Virginia, July 6th, 1876.

The Opposition in the South to the Free School System (pamphlet), address delivered before American Social Service Association at Saratoga, September 6th, 1877.

The War of Races at the South, editorial, Manchester (Va.) Courier, September 12th, 1874.

The Confederate Soldier, talk delivered at a banquet of the Association of the Army of Northern Virginia, November, 1876.

Industrial

The Prosperity of France, editorial in Richmond Daily Enquirer, February 29th, 1876.

Finance and Banking, review of Walter Bagehot's Lombard Street, a description of the Money Market, Richmond (Va.) Enquirer, November 23rd, 1873.

The Currency, editorial, Richmond (Va.) Enquirer, November 11th, 1874.

Liberal Discounts—the true Policy for Banks, article in Richmond (Va.) Enquirer, November 21st, 1873.

Our Muddy Water, signed "Citizen", article in Richmond (Va.) Enquirer, July, 1873.

The Southern Industrial Prospect, Harper's New Monthly Magazine, March, 1876.

Welcome to the Men of the West, speech printed in the Richmond (Va.) May 12th, 1877.

The Railroad Interests of Richmond, editorial in the Manchester (Va.) Courier, September 19th, 1874.

Railroads, the Arteries and Veins of the Body Politic, editorial in Manchester (Va.) Courier, April 10th, 1872.

Political

Nationalization, a speech delivered before Hood's Brigade, at Waco, Texas, June 27th, 1877.

Government notes, (in script) local and centralized.

The Political Problem in the United States, (in script) April, 1877.

Communism (in script), 1878.

The Future of the South, address delivered at the reunion of the Hampton Legion in Columbia, S.C., July 21st, 1875. Also speech delivered in Charleston, S.C., July 26th, 1875.

Morrill

The New South, article in script.

The Third Term Discussion, editorial in Manchester (Va.) Courier, Saturday, August 22nd, 1874.

The Louisiana Trouble and the Third Term Movement, editorial in the Manchester (Va.) Courier, September 26th, 1874.

The Conservative Party of Virginia—Can it Not be Nationalized? Manchester (Va.) Courier, August 29th, 1874.

Sell Not Our Birthright for a Mess of Pottage, Manchester (Va.) Courier, September 5th, 1874.

Reconciliation, Retrenchment and Reform, Richmond Daily Enquirer, January 27th, 1876.

The Centennial Appropriation in Congress, Richmond Daily Enquirer, January 27th, 1876.

The Opportunity of the Democrats, editorial in Richmond Daily Enquirer, 1876.

The Apprehended Danger of Caesarism, editorial, Manchester (Va.) Courier, October 3rd, 1874.

General T.M. Logan's tribute to Lee, News Leader, Richmond, Va., January 19th, 1909, copied from the Columbia, S.C. speech of July 21st, 1875.

General Joe Johnston, speech seconding General Johnston's nomination for Congress. Printed in the Richmond (Va.) State, August 28th, 1876.

The Arraignment of the Republican Party, editorial in the Manchester (Va.) Courier, October 3rd, 1874.

The Democratic Party and the Currency Question, editorial in the Richmond (Va.) Enquirer, November 17th, 1874.

Mr. Kelly's 3-65 Convertible Bond Bill, editorial in Richmond (Va.) Enquirer, December 13th, 1874.

From Books
General Logan's Own Writings

The Military Operations of General Beauregard, by Alfred Roman, Harper & Brothers, New York, 1883, Vol. 2, pp 557-560. Description of the Battle of Drury's Bluff. (Some books spell this Drewry's Bluff).

The Southern Student's Handbook of Reading and Oratory, A.S. Barnes & Co., New York, Chicago and New Orleans, 1879, pp 34 and 146. (One article)

Recent Newspaper Articles Concerning General Logan's Life by Lily Logan Morrill

The Logans, Recollections of a Richmond in the Days After the War. Times-Dispatch, Richmond, Virginia, August 15th, 1937.

Morrill

General Logan, C.S.A. The News and Courier, Charleston, S.C., Sunday Morning, March 3rd, 1940.

Sherman's Burning of Columbia. The News and Courier, Charleston, S.C., Sunday Morning, March 10th, 1940.

Old Views Applicable Today (From General Logan's writings.) The News and Courier, Charleston, S.C., Sunday Morning, March 17th, 1940.

Endnotes

i   From family poem or miniature epic, for Lizzie's Album by Samuel Logan, M.D., New Orleans, Picayune Print, 66 Camp Street, 1887. This was published by Mrs. E.J. Nicholson, a pioneer among women editors in the United States.

ii   From a record of the Logan family, by George William Logan, 1874. New edition by Lily Logan Morrill, 1923.

iii   Most of this college material comes from a letter written March 24th, 1933, by C.W. Hutson, an artist of New Orleans. He was a friend and classmate of T.M. Logan. Hutson served under Logan in the War Between the States, and has generously contributed much information and many letters for use in this biography.

iv   Eve of Conflict, George Fort Milton, Houghton-Mifflin C., 1934, page 435.

v   From a pamphlet, entitle "Reception of General T.M. Logan", Charleston, South Carolina, printed July 26th1875, by Comrades of the Washington Light Infantry, July, 1875. The News and Courier Job Presses, 1875. The description is by Colonel Zimmerman Davis, who commanded the Fifth Regiment of South Carolina Cavalry, Logan's Brigade.

vi. From a War Correspondence belonging to Charles Woodward Hutson (lent with permission for use).

vii. "From a letter dated June 29th, 1861, written by Mrs. George Howe, wife of the Reverend Dr. George Howe, Professor in the Presbyterian Theological Seminary at Columbia, to Mrs. W.F. Hutson."

viii. From a letter of C.W. Hutson to his father and mother written July 22nd, 1861, from the University at Charlottesville, Virginia.

ix. During the afternoon, a captain sent word to General Beauregard that he saw a column approaching, but could not distinguish the flag—so closely did the Stars and Stripes resemble the Stars and Bars! After that it was decided to have the Confederate Bars diagonal (criss-cross) instead of horizontal. My authority is the Confederate Scrap-Book, published for the benefit of the Memorial Bazaar, held in Richmond, April 11th, 1893. The particulars about T.M. Logan are from the C.W. Hutson correspondence.

x. From C.W. Hutson's letter, July 26th, 1861, from Camp at Manassas, Virginia. "I have a feeling of gladness all the time now not only at our great and truly wonderful success and the glorious name which the Legion has won for itself, but also at the almost miraculous safety of my dear friends and comrades."

xi. Much of the description of camp and army life is from the unpublished Hutson War Correspondence.

xii. From an interview with Major William A. Watts, by W.W. Ball, Editor of the News and Courier, Charleston, S.C., November 27th, 1932. Sent in a letter to Mrs. H.D. Bruns.

xiii. From Edgefield Advertiser, Edgefield, S.C., January 30th, 1879. See also My Confederate Girlhood, the memoirs of Kate Virginia Cox Logan, edited her daughter, Lily Logan Morrill, Garrett & Massie Inc., Richmond, 1932. Page 139.

xiv. From an unpublished sketch by Georgie Logan deSaussure, entitled "For My Children—Some Days of Mother's Life." Written 1921.

xv. See Note XIII.

xvi. From a letter advocating Logan's promotion from Senior Colonel to Brigadier General. Written to General S. Cooper, A.I.S. General, Richmond, Virginia, by General Longstreet. Dated December 13th, 1864. See also Battles and Leaders of the Civil War, Century Company, 1884-8, vol. 3 p. 746.

xvii. Lieutenant S.E. Welch, Co. H, afterwards Adjutant of H. Legion, C. Infantry. From Richmond Times Dispatch, July 28th, 1875.

xviii. See General Logan's letter in The Military Operations of General Beauregard, Vol. II, by Alfred Roman, Harper & Brothers, New York, 1883. See also Battles and Leaders of the Civil War, Century Company, 1884-8, vol. 4 p. 200 and 208.

xix. Edgefield Advertiser (and numerous other sources)

xx. Confederate Scrap Book, published for the benefit of the Memorial Bazaar, April 11th, 1893, Richmond, Va., I.L. Hill Printing Co. 1893, page 136.

xxi. Later came General T.M. Logan's Tribute to Lee at the Reunion of the Hampton Legion, Columbia, S.C., July 21st, 1875. This speech was much reviewed. Even as late as January 19th, 1909, the Richmond Virginia News Leader reprinted it in part.

xxii. Education and Progress, an address delivered before the Educational Association of Virginia, July 6th, 1876.

xxiii. From a letter to General S. Cooper, January 6, 1865, signed M.C. Butler, Major General.

xxiv. Page 77-My Confederate Girlhood. "Here enters a much debated question: "Who was the youngest general in the Confederate Army?" Did that honor belong to my husband, to General Kelly, or to Felix Robertson? Logan was born seven months after Kelly, both of them in 1840, but Kelly was commissioned brigadier-general on November 16, 1863, when he was twenty-three and a half, while my husband did not receive his colonel's commission until May 19, 1864, six months after Kelly had been raised to the higher grade; and Logan was not elevated to be a brigadier-general until after he was twenty-four, which would have meant after November 3, 1864. Therefore, while it is fair to say Logan was the youngest man in the service who became a general, inasmuch as he was born after both Kelly and Felix Robertson, he was not the youngest when he became general. The Confederates, in the after-years, were very precise in distinctions about matters of this sort." (Kate Virginia Cox Logan). See also Richmond Dispatch, August 12th, 1914, and article from Club Life, New York, 1879, July.

xxv. A summing up of T.M. Logan's promotions: Shortly after the surrender of Fort Sumter, Logan aided in organizing Company A, Hampton Legion, and was elected Lieutenant. The following September, he was made Captain for "great bravery". At Sharpsburg, he was cited and promoted Major in September, 1862. A few months later in January he became Lieutenant Colonel and in May, 1864, a Colonel. The next February, 1865, Logan was appointed Brigadier-General of Cavalry, in one sense the youngest Confederate officer to hold that appointment. Copies of numerous letters recommending promotion are in possession of the author. (My Confederate Girlhood, p. 66)

xxvi. From The Confederate Soldier, a speech delivered at the Association of the Army of Northern Virginia, November, 1876.

xxvii. From the speech by Colonel Zimmerman Davis at the reception to General Logan given by the Washington Light Infantry, Charleston, S. C., July 26th, 1875.

xxviii. From the Edgefield Advertiser, Edgefield, S.C. January 30th, 1879, and other sources.

xxix. From The Story of the Confederacy, by Robert Self Henry, copyright, 1931. Used by special permission of the publishers, The Bobbs-Merrill Co. Page 469.

xxx. My Confederate Girlhood, p. 77.

xxxi. Several instances in this chapter are taken from a handwritten war account of General Logan by a comrade in arms, written from Headquarters, South Carolina Division U.C.V. Aiken, S.C.

xxxii. My Confederate Girlhood, p. 79. Letter from Lily Logan to General T.M. Logan, March 2nd, 1865.

xxxiii. From an unpublished sketch by Georgie Logan deSaussure, entitled "For My Children—Some Days of Mother's Life." Written 1921.

xxxiv. An autobiography of William P. de Saussure, in pamphlet form, printed 1929.

xxxv. My Confederate Girlhood, pp. 69-76. R.E. Lee, A Biography, by Douglas Freeman, Charles Scribner's Sons, N.Y., 1935, volume 4, pp 60-61. Times-Dispatch, Sunday Magazine Section, November 22, 1936, an article by Rose Trueheart, quoting from My Confederate Girlhood on same subject of Lee's Dinner at Clover Hill.

xxxvi. Clover Hill is in Chesterfield County, Virginia. For history of this county, see the History of Chesterfield County, Notes on Addresses by Edwin P. Cox at Chesterfield Court House, September 11th, 1936. In regard to General Logan's mare, Virgie, it is interesting to note that a companion during many battles Colonel Reuben Beverly Boston, was equally fond of horses. At the very end of the war, April 6th, 1865, Colonel Boston was killed at High Bridge near Farmville, Virginia. A brother, Dr. Dudley Boston, from then until his death, always kept two horses, one named "Johnnie Reb", after his brother, and one named "Logan", after General Logan. The former horse was a grey, the latter bay. When one died, he could get another and gave it the same name, according to Dr. Boston's niece, Mrs. Dabney Minor Trice, of Charlottesville, Va.

xxxvii. The Opposition in the South to the Free School System, a paper read before American Social Service Association at Saratoga, September 6th, 1877, the subject under discussion being "The Question of Education in the Southern States."

xxxviii. My Confederate Girlhood, p. 25

xxxix. Richmond, Virginia in Old Prints, 1737-1887, Alexander Wilbourne Weddell, Johnson Publishing Co., Richmond, Va.,1932.

xl. Railroads, the Arteries and Veins of the Body Politic, editorial in Manchester (Va.) Courier, April 10th, 1872.

xli. The Apprehended Danger of Caesarism, editorial, Manchester (Va.) Courier, October 3rd, 1874. This chapter and many of General Logan's notes show interesting parallels between the 1870's and the 1930's.

xlii. From oration by General T.M. Logan at the Reunion of the Hampton Legion, Washington Light Infantry, July 21st, 1875, in Columbia, S.C. From a pamphlet published by his friends in Charleston, S.C. Walker, Evans and Cogswell, Printers, Charleston, S.C., 1875.

xliii. From a speech called the Nationalization of America delivered before the Association of Hood's Texas Brigade, at Waco, Texas, June 27th, 1877. New York Herald, June 27th, 1877. "General Logan's address was received with marked approval and frequent applause. At its conclusion the United States flag was present to the Association, and was received with three hearty and rousing cheers."

xliv. From General Logan's notebooks.

xlv. The Prosperity of France, Editorial, the Enquirer, February 29th, 1873

xlvi. The Currency, General Logan's editorial, Richmond (Va.) Enquirer, November 11th, 1874.

xlvii. Mr. Kelly's 3-65 Convertible Bond Bill, editorial in Richmond (Va.) Enquirer, December 13th, 1874.

xlviii. From letters of Judge Edwin P. Cox of Chesterfield County, Virginia to Lily Logan Morrill. Most of the coal mine material is from this source. Judge Cox was for many years Speaker of the Virginia Assembly and Judge of the Circuit Court.

xlix. Judge Logan died in 1876. He was buried in the old St. Phillip's Churchyard near the graves of his ancestors and under the monument he had so lovingly erected to his mother. His daughter Lily describes him thus: "All who knew him recognized his rare and beautiful nature . . . To us motherless ones he was mother and father in care and tenderness. My life was made by him. His ambition for me and for his other children was boundless. I well remember, when a young girl, he persuaded me to take up Hebrew (which he read easily) and he got up early every morning to give me instruction in that language. He read and studied continually and was so correct in his knowledge of scientific and other varied subjects that persons studiously inclined came to him often in order to settle doubtful and intricate questions. Yet in spite of his erudition and mental superiority, he was as simple in manners as a child, always courtly, courteous, polished and gentle, with so modest a demeanor that few were fully aware of his deep learning." Logan Record.

l. Richmond, Virginia in Old Prints, 1737-1887, Alexander Wilbourne Weddell, Johnson Publishing Co., 1932.

li. The Columbia, South Carolina Daily Union Herald for July 22nd, 1875, quoted in Manchester (Va.) Courier, July 31st, 1875.

lii. "Palmetto," writing from Charleston, S.C. to Richmond Dispatch, for July 28th, 1875, Palmetto is a pseudonym for Lieutenant S.E. Welch, Company H., and former Adjutant for Washington Light Infantry.

liii. Waco, Texas Examiner, June 27th, 1877 (Evening Edition).

liv. From General Logan's notebooks.

lv. From General Logan's notebooks.

lvi. From General Logan's notebooks.

lvii. From the Conservative Party of Virginia, Manchester, Va. Courier, August 29th, 1874, editorial.

lviii. From a letter dated March 29th, 1934, sent to Lily Logan Morrill by J.J. Bennett, of C&O Ry. Enclosed was a memorandum entitled: EXCURSION OF WESTERN BUSINESS MEN TO VIRGINIA, NORTH CAROLINA AND SOUTH CAROLINA, MAY, 1877.

lix. Men of the West. Front page headliner, Richmond (Va.) State. May 12th, 1877. Richmond Enquirer, May 14th, 1877.

lx. Richmond (Va.) News Leader, February 11th, 1929. (Justice)

lxi. Richmond (Va.) News Leader, February 11th, 1929. (Justice)

lxii. Financial Record, November 20th 1886., Washington Critic, November 22nd, 1886., Charleston (S.C.) Sunday News, December 12th, 1886., The Hour, November 20th, 1886. (See also): Richmond News Leader, (Va.) August 12th, 1914., New York Mail and Express, November 27th, 1886., Dictionary of American Biography, Charles Scribner's Sons, New York. Bibliography at the end of this book.

lxiii. The State, Richmond, Va., November 26th, 1886.

lxiv. Richmond Dispatch, November 21st and 23rd, 1886; Richmond News Leader, (Va.), February 11th, 1886; Baltimore American, November 20th, 1886; Financial Record, November 20th, 1886; Cincinnati Enquirer, November 30th, 1886.

lxv. Washington Critic, November 22nd, 1886; New York Herald, November 21st, 1886; The State, Richmond, Va., November 24th, 1886; Atlanta Constitution, November 26th, 1886; The Investigator, November 30th, 1886; Cincinnati Enquirer, November 30th, 1886.

lxvi. From a pamphlet called History of the Telautograph.

lxvii. Dr. Henry Dickson Bruns was born in Charleston, S.C., 1859; died New Orleans, 1932. Educated at the University of Virginia. Was surgeon in charge at the Eye, Ear, Nose and Throat Hospital of New Orleans, 1893-1930. For many years he lectured on Ophthalmology at Tulane University Medical School, and at the time of his death headed the list of professors emeriti. He was a pathologist at Charity Hospital, New Orleans, for many years. He was interested in social and political affairs all his life. Led in the famous anti-lottery campaign of Louisiana, took the stump for woman's suffrage, was altogether for clean and honest government and constructive reforms. He made many valuable contributions to medical literature.

lxviii. Dictionary of American Biography, Scribner's.

lxix. Dictionary of American Biography, Scribner's

lxx. From pamphlet called History of the Telautograph.

lxxi. Richmond Dispatch, December 31st, 1867.

lxxii. The Railroad Interests of Richmond, editorial in the Manchester (Va.) Courier, September 19th, 1874. For other editorials on this subject see last pages of Bibliography.

lxxiii. For list of editorials, see last pages of Bibliography.

lxxiv. Speeches can also be found near the end of the Bibliography. Titles only. Chapter IX is on Nationalization.

lxxv. See Chapters XII and XIII.